M000222819

OUR SERVICE OUR STORIES

Indiana Veterans Recall Their World War II Experiences

RONALD P. MAY

PRINTED IN THE UNITED STATES OF AMERICA

TABLE OF CONTENTS

Foreword

As a newspaper editor, I get a lot of submissions from people who think they can make a few bucks for almost no work. They generally don't last more than a month before giving up.

So, when I first saw the email from Ron May with his pitch to write stories about veterans, I was skeptical. I thought, *What a great topic, but will this guy actually be able to pull it off?*

He has done that and much more, including winning several awards in the annual Hoosier State Press Association Better Newspaper Contest. Our first agreement was for one story a month about a local veteran. Ron ramped that up when we asked him for more and often writes three stories a month for us now.

Our readers love his features and they often tell us just that. That love comes from seeing the care he gives each and every subject.

The person he is interviewing isn't just the next story, they are a veteran who lived a piece of history that needs to be recorded. The veteran, through Ron's writing, becomes a hero and an inspiration for generations to come.

It is exciting to see these stories leap from the pages of our newspaper, and in many cases to the pages of this book, too. My hope is that Ron will be able to reach even more people and record even more stories as a result of publishing *Our Service, Our Stories*. Because, while 36 profiles is a good start, there are thousands more whose wartime exploits can be brought to life through Ron's excellent storytelling.

I hope you enjoy this book as much as I have enjoyed having Ron write for my newspaper.

Brian Culp, Editor
Martinsville Reporter-Times
Mooresville-Decatur Times

PHOTO BY KARLIE ANN MAY

Prelude

This year marks the 70th Anniversary of the conclusion of World War II in 1945 (Victory in Europe on May 8th and Victory in Japan on August 14th/15th). Of the 16 million service members who fought in World War II, it is estimated that only 855,000 are still alive today. And those survivors are dying off at a rate of almost 500 each day. As they die, not only do we lose the men and women who served, we lose the stories of their military service unless they have already been preserved in some format. The rush is on to capture as many of their stories as possible, while some of them are still with us.

Morgan County Veterans Memorial in Martinsville, IN.

Introduction

In March of 2012 I found myself in a career transition. I had spent the last 22 years as a pastor and had just concluded a long ministry with no further church prospects on the horizon. I was having a conversation with my sister Linda, who was visiting me and my family. Linda and I were sitting in my den when the subject of what I should do next came up.

I shared with my sister that I had thought about a very different type of career. I had spent much of my professional life preaching from the pulpit about the stories recorded in the Bible, and I was wondering what it would be like to write about the life stories of people — especially the service stories of our military veterans. In my years as a pastor I had always enjoyed visiting with and honoring the veterans of the congregations that I was serving. I found myself fascinated by their military service and would often, upon their deaths, incorporate a little bit of their military service stories into their funeral messages.

My own military service also prompted me toward this pursuit. I had spent 22 years as a Navy Reserve Chaplain; and had been privileged to serve ten different military units. As I was nearing the end of my career I wanted to maintain a connection to the military culture and to those who had served.

So, as I shared all of this with my sister she said to me, "You should do it, Ron. I think you would do a great job with that!" My interest and her encouragement motivated me to explore the matter further.

I recruited three veterans from the congregation that I had recently served and asked their permission to interview them and write a story about their military service. The three veterans were Chuck Bowling, Paul Maves and Herman Strakis. Chuck served during the Korean War. Paul and Herman were World War II veterans.

I soon added another veteran subject to my writing exploration — Carl Marsh (also a member of my former church). Carl's story was a bit more challenging, as he had already died before I started writing. Thankfully, he had shared enough of his military service story with me and with his family before his death that I was able to piece together his story.

I subsequently added a fourth World War II veteran, Arthur Brown as another story subject.

After completing each of their stories I reflected on the accomplishment. I found the work of writing their stories to be stimulating and very fulfilling. And the veterans and their families seemed to be pleased with the product as well.

But something was still missing in the experience for me. I wanted to do more than just write their military stories for them and their families. I also wanted to have their stories be read by others — especially the members of their community. I felt that by making their stories accessible to others I could honor them as well as educate and inspire people by their service to our country.

With that goal in mind I began to write to the editors of local county newspapers in the Indianapolis area asking whether or not they would be willing to print veteran service stories that I wanted to submit to them. I also asked if they would pay me for the stories, as I was in need of making a living.

Brian Culp, the editor of the *Martinsville Reporter Times* and *Mooresville-Decatur Times* newspapers in Morgan County, Indiana was the first to respond to my inquiry. He said he was interested. We talked about article content, length, format and frequency. And by July of 2012 I had submitted my first veteran story. That started a relationship with Brian that continues today. I regularly submit articles of Morgan County Veterans for publication in his newspapers. Not only does he print the articles, he puts them on prime newspaper real estate — the front page!

Some months after I started writing for the newspapers in Morgan County, I submitted a story to the *Hendricks County Flyer*. Editor Kathy Linton was kind enough to print it, and soon she began publishing my service stories of Hendricks County veterans.

The readers' response to these stories was very favorable. I began receiving periodic notes and phone calls thanking me for the stories and, at times, offering me the names of other potential story subjects.

The idea of publishing these stories in a book arose sometime during that first year of writing. I realized that a book format would preserve the stories much longer and expand the potential audience of readers.

I kept interviewing and writing for another year as I waited to accumulate more veteran stories for the book. I then began to talk to others about the idea of publishing. Brian Culp informed me of a local publisher in Martinsville. I met with Robin Surface of Fideli Publishing and shared my book idea with her. Before long, she was showing me format and layout options.

I decided to make each veteran story a separate chapter in the book and expand what I had earlier written about the veteran in the newspaper article. In all cases, there was more to each of their stories than what I could include in the articles due to space restrictions. And I usually had more photos of them than what appeared in the article. So, I had what I needed to expand their stories.

Because I set out to write a book about World War II veterans, I did not include Chuck Bowles' service story during the Korean War in this volume. Nor did I include any of the other 15 veterans of different wars and eras that I have written articles about over the past two years. I hope to write a future volume on the stories of these veterans.

It will also be obvious to the reader that all of my veteran subjects are men. This was not so much by design as it was the outcome of limited opportunity. I am well aware of the very significant contributions made by the over 350,000 women who served as Nurses, WAVES, WAC's, USMC Women's Reserve, Coast Guard SPARS, Red Cross Volunteers, Entertainers, and Rosie the Riveters back on the home front. However, it is only more recently that I have come into personal contact with some of these women. It is my intent to include their stories in a future volume.

The reader will notice that the stories of Arthur Brown, Carl Marsh, Paul Maves and Herman Strakis are twice as long as the other veteran stories in this book. The reason for the discrepancy is that the stories I wrote of them did not start out as articles but rather as complete histories of their service years. I spent much more time interviewing them and learning about their experiences during military service and their lives afterwards. The length of their stories reflects that breadth of information they shared with me. I decided against shortening their stories to match the length of the other veteran stories in the book in favor of sharing all of what I came to know about them.

I used the same information gathering process for each veteran that I interviewed. I visited them in their homes and asked questions about their life and service, recording their responses on a digital recorder. I recorded each interview not only so that I could remember the veteran's response but also so that I could print the exact words of the veteran for direct quotes. In some cases, in an effort to preserve the style and voice of the veteran, I chose not to make grammatical corrections to their sentences.

I also made a decision early on to accept each veteran's memory of the events connected with his time of service without trying to verify the accuracy of the details. Memory is imperfect for any of us. The combination of advanced age and the timing of events that took place over 70 years ago are bound to produce some inaccuracies. I accepted that, and I hope the readers will as well. This is a book about *their* stories, which, for me, means that **their** memories of the events are more important than what may have actually happened.

I scanned as many of the veterans' photos as I could to use in their stories. Some had more photos and some had less. A few veterans had no photos at all of their time of service. I used whatever I received, and I added other photographs from the internet — mostly ones taken by military members and, as such, within the public domain. Every effort was made to make sure that I used only public domain photographs. In the event that I inadvertently infringed on someone's copyrighted work, I offer my apology.

Because my primary interest was preserving as much of the "voice" of each veteran's story as possible I have intentionally used frequent and sometimes large quotes in the stories. I have tried to add as little as possible to each story. I saw my job more as an interviewer who asked the questions, recorded the replies and arranged the material in a presentable format. My own contributions are limited to presenting each story under a title/theme and providing some historical background on battles, planes, ships or other equipment.

My writing venture has taken me into the homes or rooms of each of these 36 veterans. And my life has been enriched by spending time with them. I was touched and inspired greatly by these men as I listened to their stories and sought to preserve them. This book is my small way of thanking and honoring them for the privilege of getting to know them. And it is my way of expressing gratitude for their selfless sacrifice and dedicated service to our country in a time of national threat and world upheaval.

None of these veterans thought of themselves as heroes. They were humble and self-effacing, preferring that I would have interviewed someone else instead of them. Most of them mentioned that the 'real heroes' were the men who died while serving their country. Some veterans declined my request for an interview, even after repeated attempts. I respected their decisions but mourned the loss of preserving their stories.

In speaking to each of the veterans, I tried to make a case for preserving their service story. I told them that they are the last voices to give "I was there" details and meaning to the World War II experience. I told them that they speak for those who are no longer able to speak for themselves — for dead buddies that died on the battle field or for other veterans who came back home from the war but died before ever sharing their stories. I told them they speak to future generations that need to be reminded of our nation's contribution and sacrifice toward preserving freedom in our country and abroad. And I told them that their stories may well inspire others toward military and/or other public service.

Such stories of sacrifice, duty, honor and commitment have always been part of the rich fabric of our nation's history — a tapestry to which future generations will add their threads of patriotism and public service for our great country.

I thank you, the readers, for taking the time to read these stories. If you are touched and inspired by their service and their lives I will consider this book to have been a great success.

INDY HONOR FLIGHT

At the same time that I was beginning to write veteran stories I also stumbled upon an organization called "Indy Honor Flight". I learned that it was a non-profit organization, part of the national 'Honor Flight Network', created solely to honor Indiana's veterans for all their sacrifices. Indy Honor Flight transports senior veterans to Washington, D.C. on an all-expense paid trip to visit and reflect at their memorials. Throughout the day, the veterans receive much deserved expressions of gratitude from the public.

I attended the meet and greet the evening prior to their first flight in September of 2012 and met the executive director, Grant Thompson. I explained a little bit to him that I had begun writing military service stories and asked if I could be involved in some way. He invited me to follow him around and continue our conversation as he took care of last minute preparations for the event.

I soon found myself fascinated by the organization and inspired by Grant's energy and devotion in getting as many Indiana veterans as possible to Washington D.C. to experience their memorial. I quickly became a volunteer and served for a few years as the organization's media and communications representative.

With my desire to preserve veteran stories and Grant's desire to honor them with a trip to Washington D.C., I saw a wonderful opportunity for a partnership. As more and more veterans signed up with Indy Honor Flight for the trip, Grant

Indy Honor Flight Veteran Reflects at WWII Memorial.

and I began exploring how we might preserve the stories of these veterans. An effort is already underway to recruit interviewers and writers to capture the stories of these brave men and women from the "greatest generation" and post them to the Indy Honor Flight website.

In April of 2015 Indy Honor Flight hosted its tenth trip to Washington D.C., taking two hundred veterans to see their memorials and be honored by a grateful public. In less than three years this incredible organization has taken 835 World War II and Korean veterans to our nation's capital to be honored.

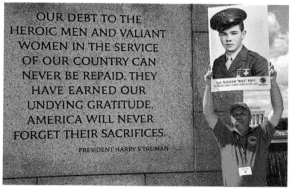

Grant Thompson holding the portrait of his late grandfather, Cpl. Bill Pace.

As a strong supporter of Indy Honor Flight I will make a donation to the organization for every book sold.

For more information visit their website : www.indyhonorflight.org or find them on Facebook.

Indiana Veterans Gather by the State Marker of the WWII Memorial.

Veteran Receives Welcome Home from Trip.

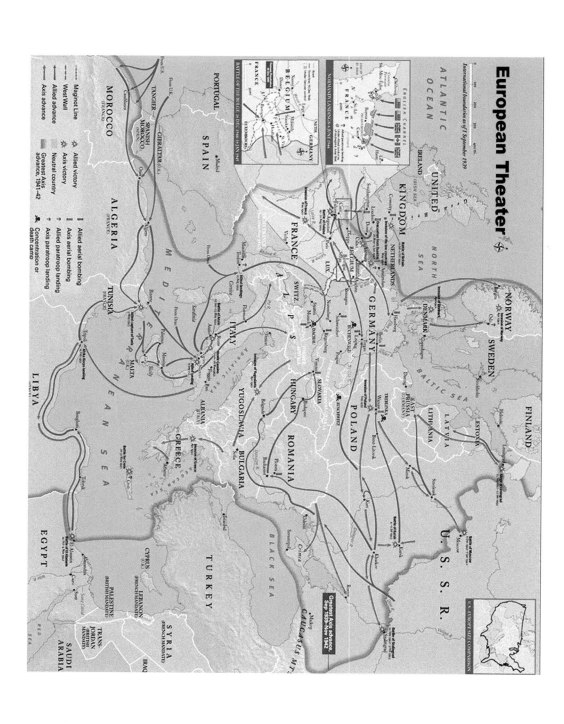

European Theater

International boundaries as of 1 September 1939

EUROPEAN THEATER

Butcher in the Meat Grinder
Soldier Survives the Grind of Combat

Bill Brummett was a butcher for most of his working years. But for a few months in 1945 he felt like he was the one in the meat grinder.

Born on July 6, 1926 in Martinsville, Indiana, Charles William Brummett was the middle child of twelve children raised by his parents Dewey and Susie Brummett.

Brummett got his first job as a butcher in Indianapolis at the age of 16. It was to be a lifelong career for him.

In October of 1944, he was drafted into the Army at the age of 18. Brummett completed his basic training as an infantryman at Fort McClellan, Alabama.

By January of 1945, he was on his way to the European theater of war. He was assigned to Company I of the 47th Regiment, 9th Army Division, which was pushing its way across Germany toward victory.

Part of a massive Army movement across Germany from March through May, Brummett recalled that initially there wasn't too much resistance because the Germans were falling back to Berlin as fast as they could.

Brummett remembered the cold. "It was still winter time," he said. "We either slept outside or in a house for a few hours of sleep each night."

Allied planes continued bombing major cities with the Army going in and cleaning up what was left.

But combat became more intense as the division came closer to Berlin. Brummett felt like he was in a meat grinder. "We went through the countryside with the tanks", recalled Brummett. "We'd clean out the town and move on to the next one. It was one nightmare after another!"

Map of Allied advance across Germany.

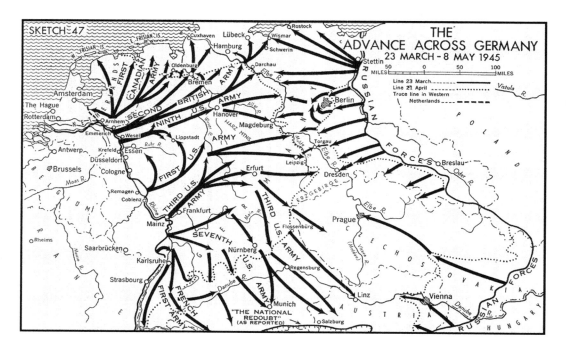

One of those nightmares happened early on in his combat experience. As his unit was moving forward, a soldier behind him was shot and went down. Brummett picked up the man's .30 caliber machine gun and used the weapon for the rest of the war. It was designed for two men, but he operated it by himself. "It put out a lot of lead," Brummett said.

And it's a good thing that it did! During the last two weeks of the war Brummett saved the life of one of his Army buddies with a one round shot from his machine gun. "I see the old man going down, like in a slow motion picture; blood going everywhere," Brummett said sadly, referring to the German soldier he killed in order to save his buddy.

His buddy, a logger from California named 'Pop', told Brummett, following the shot that saved his life, "Kid, I'll never call you kid again!"

Brummett was involved in the well-known battle at Remagen, a railroad bridge across the Rhine River. The Germans blew the bridge just after Brummett and his unit had crossed it. He earned one of his two bronze stars during that battle.

The Allies kept pushing forward toward Berlin where the final blow would come against the Germans. Brummett recalled, "We got to 12 kilometers of Berlin, and that's where Hitler killed himself. After he killed himself the Germans just gave up all at once."

After Germany's surrender, Brummett's unit moved south to Dachau, Germany — the sight of the first Nazi concentration

Brummet holding a VFW plaque recognizing his service.

camp in Germany where Jews were imprisoned. While there, Brummett was discharged from the Army.

Not having accumulated enough points to return home at the war's end, Brummett next joined the Army Air Forces and returned to his butcher roots by doing some cooking in LeHarve, France for a few weeks.

He continued cooking as he got on a Liberty ship for his return trip home across the Atlantic. Needing to finish out the final months of his enlistment, Brummett reported to Lake Charles, Louisiana where he served as a chauffeur for one of the Generals. He then reported to Biggs Field in El Paso, Texas for the last couple months. He was discharged in December 1945 and made it home to Indiana one day after Christmas in 1945.

Brummett returned to his job as a butcher at Kroger and started the next chapter of his life.

On August 19, 1948, Brummett married Lavinna Croell. Their marriage was blessed with 7 children — 3 girls and 4 boys.

In 1950, Brummett returned to military service. He was called up by the Air National Guard in support of the Korean conflict. This time, instead of being in the meat grinder of combat, he operated one at a U.S. base chow hall in Japan. He was put in charge of the meat for all the air bases in Japan and supplied meat to an Army Air base in Korea. Brummett served for a year and returned home in 1951.

He went back to Kroger and continued his craft behind the meat counter, a post that he held for the next 20 years.

In 1970, Brummett and his family moved to New Smyrna Beach, Florida. The long-time butcher turned to the sea and began a 15-year career in cutting wood and building flat bottom shrimp boats. He also kept active in the local VFW and American Legion, serving as Post Commander of each.

The Brummett's returned to Indiana in the late 1980's. In 2011, his beloved Lavinna died. The couple had been married for 63 years. Two of his sons also died in tragic motorcycle accidents. In addition to his surviving five children, he has been blessed with many grandchildren and lot of great friends!

Brummett died on August 15, 2014. He was 88 years old.

Life on the Bridges
Veteran Guards and Later Builds Bridges

Bridges have figured prominently in the life of Lewis Collier. During World War II he crossed them and helped guard them as his division pushed into Germany. Later in life he helped build them over stretches of I-465 in Indianapolis.

Collier was born on March 2, 1923 and grew up in Washington City, Indiana near Salem. He worked on a farm with his dad and later was hired by a hog farmer.

When all of his buddies started enlisting in the service in the early 1940s, Collier decided to do the same. He chose the patriotic date of July 4, 1942 and signed up with the U.S. Army.

He traveled to Alabama for his

LEWIS "LOU" COLLIER
US ARMY, PROUD WWII VETERAN

basic training. "It was rough," Collier recalled of the training. And it was made a lot rougher for him when he sustained a foot injury halfway through and had to drop out of his platoon to undergo rehabilitation. (He broke four of his toes while running.) What was meant to be a couple of months of training turned into a whole year before Collier finally healed up, repeated the training, and graduated from boot camp.

After a short furlough home, Collier returned to the Army and was assigned to Company L of the 406ᵗʰ Battalion, 102ⁿᵈ Infantry Division. The division was known as the "Ozark Division" because many of the units were originally made up of men from the Ozark region of Arkansas and Missouri. It became part of Patton's Army.

In September of 1944, the division boarded the Queen Elizabeth troop transport ship in New York City and headed off to war!

During the trip to Europe, a German U-boat pursued them until an Allied plane dropped a depth charge on it. Twelve days later Collier and the division were across the Atlantic Ocean and in LeHarve, France.

The division traveled across Northern France and through Belgium defeating the remaining pockets of German resistance and mopping up.

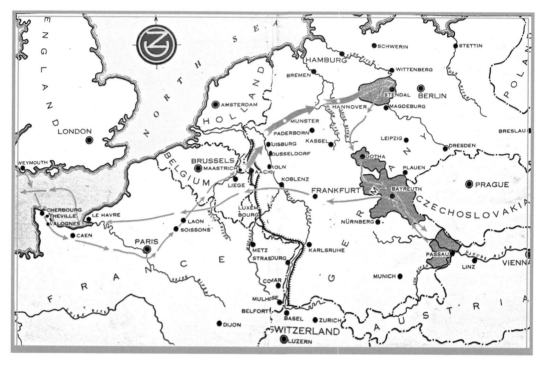

Map of 102nd Division troop movement.

Collier remembers a very different Christmas experience that year. The regular supplies were delayed in getting to them. So, for their Christmas meal, the men of the 102nd had a piece of cherry pie.

The 102nd made its way to the German-Netherlands border where Collier and the rest of the company had a close call during combat.

"We were pinned down," Collier explained about his unit's first push into Germany. "We were going up a hill with woods. We had one guy get killed."

On another combat occasion Collier was on the run toward a ditch when he came under German machine gun fire. "Before I got to the ditch — just as I jumped — the machine gunner knocked the helmet right off my head!" When he later retrieved his helmet he found 5 holes in it. "It wasn't my time," he replied with a sense of resignation and gratitude.

The division kept pushing across Northern Germany. By April of 1945 it had reached the Elbe River, 48 miles from Berlin, where the unit dug in and stayed in fox holes for 3 days waiting for the Russians to take Berlin.

The division was under strict orders to stop their advance near the bridge, which crossed the Elbe River and await the Russian Army's advance through Berlin from the East. This would be as far as most of the 102nd would go. Collier remembers some disappointment from the men that they never got to see Berlin.

On May 3, 1945, following the Russian invasion of Berlin, the members of the 102nd shook hands with the members of the Russian 156th Division, officially bringing an end to combat. Five days later, the war in Europe officially came to an end as Germany surrendered.

U.S. Forces meet Russian forces.

Germany occupation sectors.

Collier remembers well spending time along the Elbe River guarding the bridge and waiting for the arrival of the Russians. When he wasn't guarding the bridge he was permitted to hunt for food. Deer were his favorite target. He figures he probably killed 25 or more during his time traversing France, Belgium and Germany. And the fresh meat was always a welcome treat for the men of his unit.

After combat ended, Collier was assigned occupation duty in Germany. He was responsible for guarding one of the river crossings. The U.S. sector was on one side of the river and the Russian sector was on the other side of the river.

And guards from both sectors sometimes met in the middle of the bridge for conversation, friendship, and some black market business. "The Russians bought cigarettes from us and paid us a lot of money," Collier remembered.

After some months of occupation duty Collier found himself on another troop transport heading, this time, for Japan for the anticipated invasion. He was somewhere on the Pacific Ocean when word came of Japan's surrender, bringing a close to his combat and his chapter of life in the Army.

When Collier returned home he went back to the family farm near Salem, Indiana and worked there for several years.

Two years after his return he met and married his wife, Wilma Gilstrap, on March 3, 1948. Together they raised five children and enjoyed 65 years of marriage before her death in 2010.

When Collier was in his 40's he decided to move his family to Indianapolis and take a job with Citizens Gas and Coke Utility, where he worked for ten years. He moved on to work at the rail yard in Avon, Indiana, laying underground pipe. Two years later, he went into bridge construction work. For twelve years he helped build many of the bridges over Interstate 465 around Indianapolis.

Bridge over Elbe River.

After an almost fatal fall from scaffolding which injured his back, Collier retired from building bridges. But, he soon learned, he could not retire from working. Work was just too much a part of him to stop doing it — even after a major accident. "If I'm going to die, I'm going to die working," he said.

And so he kept on with his labors; working at a Shell service station in Danville for some years before opening a lawn mower repair shop. He would still be working now if advanced age didn't limit him. Now at the age of 92, he spends his days relaxing at his apartment in Plainfield, Indiana.

But he still gets out for monthly visits with other veterans. Collier was on the inaugural Indy Honor Flight to Washington D.C. in September of 2012. He has kept in touch with other veterans from his flight and continues to support the organization whose mission is to fly veterans out to see the memorials that have been erected in their honor.

Before ending the interview the hardworking, patriotic man said, "If war broke out again and I was young enough I would go again." Duty to country still burns brightly in that 92-year-old body. Maybe that is why he and so many others of his era are known as "the greatest generation."

Lou reviewing a book on unit history.

By Sea and By Land
Veteran Covers Vast Stretches During World War II

The battlegrounds of World War II encompassed vast stretches of real estate across parts of three continents. Walter Dreyfus knows that all too well. The Greenwood, Indiana veteran served both at sea and on land along two of those continents.

Dreyfus, who was born in 1923 in Milwaukee, Wisconsin, grew up in Birmingham, Alabama and Nashville, Tennessee before moving to Indianapolis, where he graduated from Shortridge High School (Indianapolis) in 1940. Following high school Dreyfus spent one and a half years at Butler University before moving back with his parents who had relocated to Evanston, Illinois. He joined the Navy in June of 1942. During his six weeks of boot camp at Great Lakes Naval Training Center he scored high on an aptitude test and the Navy tagged him to become a radio technician.

Following primary radio materials school at Oklahoma A&M in Stillwater and radar school at Treasure Island, California he was shipped off to North Africa in April of 1943. He was assigned to the *USS Samuel Chase,* a converted Coast Guard Assault Transport that became the headquarters ship for Admiral Hall. Dreyfus installed and maintained radio and radar equipment.

The ship carried a crew of 4,000 and could transport up to 1,200 troops. And it had lots of radio and electronic equipment! "It was a floating radio shack," said Dreyfus. "We used to kid that if they turned all the transmitters on the ship would

USS Samuel Chase.

light up." In addition to troops the ship also carried the LCVP's (Landing Craft Vehicle Personnel).

After arriving in North Africa the ship put troops ashore at Algiers for "Operation Torch" and then supported the Allied amphibious training exercises on the coast of North Africa. The Allied troops; which included Americans, French and Algerians, were preparing for the invasion of Sicily, code-named "Operation Husky" and the invasion of mainland Italy.

As the July 10th date neared for the amphibious landing, the Samuel Chase crossed the Mediterranean Sea and approached the south central shoreline of Sicily in the Gulf of Gela, which was the designated location for the Allied invasion. It anchored about two miles from shore and spent several nights there while the landings continued. During this time, the ship was subject to frequent air attacks by the German Luftwaffe night and day. "You felt like you were a sitting duck out there with flares lighting up the sky and the whole fleet being exposed as bombs are dropping," Dreyfus recalled. "It was like a fireworks display!"

During their time near Sicily, Dreyfus was recruited by the ship's chaplain to show the 8 mm movies to the men on ship. "I would show one reel to the enlisted men and then have to rewind the reel and get it up to the officer wardroom so that they could watch it too."

In September, the *USS Samuel Chase* supported the invasion of mainland Italy.

Then, in November of 1943, Dreyfus was transferred from sea to land and was assigned to the staff of Admiral John Wilkes in Plymouth, England. He traveled around southern England installing radio equipment on Minesweepers, LVTs (Landing Vehicles Tracked) and LST's (Landing Ships Tanks). He also installed

Amphibious landing.

and maintained IFF (Identification Friend or Foe) equipment on the ships, which was used as secondary radar to help identify whether approaching ships or aircraft were friendly or enemy craft.

As D-Day approached (June 6, 1944), Dreyfus and other radio techs franti-cally went from ship to ship, changing out the radio crystals that controlled the frequencies so that Germans would not intercept their radio communications.

On June 19, 1944, Dreyfus boarded the *USS Rockaway,* a sea plane tender, which transported him to Omaha Beach the following day. There Dreyfus and other Naval personnel had the unpleasant task of retrieving dead bodies still laying on the beach from the amphibious landing that had taken place two weeks ear-

Burial at sea.

lier. "We would retrieve the bodies, take the dog tags off, and then put a weight around them in a canvas bag and bury them at sea," he recalled sadly.

He also patrolled the beach and served as a communication link between Army troops in the field and the big Navy ships still anchored out in the English Channel. "I relayed to the ships the coordinates from Army units to help direct the supporting fire missions of the big guns," Dreyfus said.

For a week or so Dreyfus patrolled up and down the beach near Cherbourg, France as they waited for that city to be taken by the Allies. PT boats that needed their radios repaired would tie off to a buoy and Dreyfus would go out and fix them. "Sometimes I had to leave in the middle of the night to go out to the buoy and repair a radio in a PT boat," he recalled.

By mid-July, 1944 Dreyfus moved ashore in Cherbourg. "It was July 14th, which was Bastille Day," he recalled. "It was neat since the French were celebrating their past and their present deliverance from oppression."

Dreyfus initially went to abandoned German fortifications to recover and repair German radios that had been left behind.

In August, he was part of a reconnaissance party that got ambushed by the Germans near Saint-Malo in Brittany (France). Somehow the communications department that Dreyfus was traveling with got miles ahead of the main convoy and

Walter poses beside a Jeep.

SCR-399 radio unit Dreyfus rode in during the German's ambush near Dol, Brittany on Aug. 2, 1944.

the separated men found themselves in a pocket of German forces, outnumbered 50 to 500. The men abandoned their trucks and sought concealment in nearby ditches. "It was a scary situation," he said, remembering the shots and mortars that were aimed at them. "I hugged the ground as closely as I could," he recalled of his efforts to stay hidden. It took several hours for an Army unit to finally locate and rescue them. Dreyfus recalled that approximately 7 men were killed by the Germans during the ambush.

He stayed in Cherbourg until September 1944. During his time there, he met a woman from Indianapolis named Catherine Fox. She was in the WAC (Women's Army Corps) and was serving in Cherbourg. They went on several site-seeing trips together while they were serving near each other.

It was also during this time that Dreyfus passed the test and was promoted to Chief Petty Officer. The promotion required a change in uniforms for Dreyfus. As there were no U.S. uniform shops in France he had to fly to London to purchase what he needed for the new rank.

By September of 1944 Dreyfus was back at sea. He was transferred to LeHavre, France where he supported four Coast Guard Cutters that were watching for floating mines and were guiding supply and troop ships into and out of the port from the English Channel.

U.S.S. EARLE (DD-635) DESTROYER

Official U. S. Navy Photograph

Life on a destroyer like this is one of action and excitement every minute

Tonnage 1700 Tons	•	Armament. Main Batteries 4-5″ 38	•	Torpedo Tubes 10-21″ Quin	•	Crew 210 Men

Dreyfus returned to the U.S. in April of 1945 on a 30 day leave. In May, he was then assigned as Chief Radio Technician to the *USS Earle,* a Destroyer which had its homeport in Norfolk, VA. He became a senior petty officer as the ship was transformed into a minesweeper. The ship was in the yards when the war came to an end in Europe and in Japan.

Late in August the *USS Earle* left Norfolk and headed to Japan for minesweeping duty on the waters between Japan and Korea. Dreyfus visited Sasebo, Japan during that time.

By December of 1945, he was in the process of getting discharged. He returned to the U.S. and received his discharge from Norfolk, VA in January of 1946. He had served for 3 years and 6 months. "I was blessed to have good duty, good officers, good men to work with and lucky to not have been hurt anywhere along the way," he said.

After being discharged from the Navy, Dreyfus returned to Chicago. One weekend he traveled to Indianapolis to visit college friends and looked for Catherine

Fox, who was from Indianapolis. He came down the following weekend and every weekend after that for the next several months. They were married on July 27, 1946.

Five years after being discharged, Dreyfus was recalled to active duty for support during the Korean Conflict. This time, he didn't have to go overseas. He spent 16 months helping to train officers in radio equipment at the Glenview Naval Air Station near Chicago.

In his civilian career, Dreyfus was a salesman for a book publishing company in Chicago from 1949-1972. He was transferred to New York City and New Jersey during the decade from 1952-62 before returning to Chicago as a sales manager with the company. He then worked in the insurance business until 1993 when he retired at the age of 70.

He and his wife raised two sons: Gordon and Mark. The couple was also blessed with two grandchildren and two great-great grandchildren. Dreyfus and Catherine moved to Greenwood, Indiana in December of 2007.

Dreyfus and Catherine enjoyed traveling throughout the country and made many international trips together. They visited 21 countries and traveled through all 50 states. "My wife was a great asset to me as I traveled for business," Dreyfus recalled. "She was outgoing, gregarious, and lovable. People took to Catherine."

A few of those trips included visits back to Cherbourg, France where the couple had first met. They were there for both the 50th and 60th anniversaries of Cherbourg's liberation. They

Walter and Catherine.

Walter on his trip to the World War II memorial.

made friends there, and Dreyfus continues to correspond with some of them today.

Catherine died in August of 2013. The couple had been married for 67 years. "We had a great life together," Dreyfus said.

Dreyfus traveled to Washington DC with Indy Honor Flight in the spring of 2013 to visit the memorial erected in his honor. "It was a marvelous experience," he said. "To see the kind of welcomes that we got at Washington D.C. and at the airport (Indy) and everywhere else that we went — people coming up to us hugging and kissing and shaking your hand — it was just so overwhelming!" Among the crowd that welcomed the veterans back to Indianapolis were Dreyfus' sons (who flew in from out of state) and his wife's relatives.

Travels Across Europe
Veteran traverses France, Belgium & Germany with the 9th Army

Some people dream of traveling across Europe. Kermit Emerson of Mooresville, Indiana never dreamed of it, but he did do it — at least a major part of Northern Europe. It was no vacation though, as his travels were at the U.S. Army's direction and were during the thick of World War II.

Emerson was born in 1924 in Liberty, Kentucky (south central). He was raised on a farm and was the sixth of twelve children born to his parents, Tommy and Jennie (Monday) Emerson.

In 1941, at the age of sixteen, he came to Indiana and, through a connection to a distant relative, started working on a farm. He earned .75 cents a day and worked for two years before returning to his native Kentucky.

His time at home was short-lived as he decided to enlist in the Army in June of 1943. "My friends were already gone, and I was probably going to get drafted anyway," he recalled.

He completed his basic training at Fort Sill, Oklahoma at the Artillery Training Center. In October of 1943, he reported to Fort Ord in Monterey Bay, California where he would remain the next seven months completing his advanced training.

Emerson traveled across the country to New York in June of 1944. From there he boarded the Italian Liner turned troop transport, *SS Saternia*, and headed for

Kermit with guitar at Fort Still.

Liverpool, England. By September, he had crossed the English Channel and was in Cherbourg, France. He was part of the 9th Army, assigned to the 207th Field Artillery Battalion Service Supply Division.

Even though the Allied invasion forces had passed through France three months earlier (June of 1944), there were still pockets of German forces that had been cut off from the main body of the Nazi's retreat. It was here that Emerson had his first experience with combat.

In October of 1944, his battalion crossed France and was in Belgium, and by October 26th, they arrived in Germany. They continued their advance until they settled along the combat line between Germany and Holland. His battalion fired 8-inch howitzer artillery guns in support of the action about 10 miles to their front.

Thirty days later, the battalion was on the move again — this time entering Germany and crossing both the Rhine and Rohr Rivers near the city of Duesseldorf. Emerson's unit settled there for the next four months to give firing support to the 9th Army as it progressively diminished Nazi resistance.

"It was a long, cold winter," Emerson noted of the four months in Germany from November 1944 through April 1945.

The famous Battle of the Bulge occurred during this time frame. Emerson and his battery were spared from being tagged for the heavy action in Belgium because their 8-inch howitzers were too heavy and lacked the maneuverability that the Army needed for fast transport.

While remaining on location in Germany, his battery still fired their big guns a few times each day, just to keep them operable in the cold temperatures.

British forces were co-located near the Army's 207th field artillery. "At 9:30 am each morning the British firing would stop for tea time," Emerson jokingly recalled.

8-inch Howitzer.

When he wasn't firing the 8-inch howitzers, Emerson kept busy driving a jeep or truck on supply runs. He often drove officers to where they needed to be. And, when time permitted, he made himself useful in the kitchen, helping to cook and feed the members of his battery.

He and some of the members of his battery had come across a 14x14 block building with a basement. They found water in the basement 16 inches deep. After spending a day bailing it out, they decided to make it their new winter barracks and slept there for the next several months.

Recalling one close-call memory, Emerson shared that he was half a block from the building one day when he heard noise coming from the rubble of another building. Thinking it was a German soldier; he pointed his carbine rifle and slowly advanced. As he peeked around the corner he was relieved to find the noise was coming from a rooster scratching. "He's lucky," said Emerson! "I could have easily killed him and we would have had chicken and dumplings that evening for dinner."

The final point of advance for the 9th Army was the Elbe River, which was reached in April of 1945. This was the agreed upon demarcation point with the Russian troops that were pushing in from the east.

When the war ended in May, the 9th Army settled into some mop up work, which included collecting weapons from surrendering troops of Germany's

1st Army. "They were tickled to death to meet us," Emerson said of the German soldiers. "They were so glad it (the war) was finally over!"

There was no quick ticket home after Germany' surrender. Everyone had to wait to accumulate enough points (based on time spent in theater) to get home. Although some of the 207th began returning home as early as November of 1945, Emerson had to wait longer. He spent several months in Germany cleaning up military vehicles that were going to be shipped back to the States. He was then sent to Frankfort, Germany and assigned to another artillery battalion that had been converted to a transportation battalion. He spent his days doing jeep runs to pick up and drop off people at the Frankfort airport.

By December 2, 1945, Emerson was finally tagged to ship out for the U.S., barely making it home in time for Christmas.

"The worst part of the war experience was crossing the Atlantic in a liberty ship during the winter month," Emerson recalled. "It took 17 days to cross and 10 of those days were really bad weather with high waves."

When he finally did make it home he had been away at war for 18 months. He had left behind a very long travel swath across Northern Europe.

Emerson used his GI Bill to be trained as a bricklayer. He worked in that trade

for 18 years. He then shifted to welding as a plumber and steam fitter and worked another 18 years.

He and his wife Ruby enjoyed 53 years together before her death. They raised three children and welcomed 10 grandchildren and great-grandchildren. Emerson married his second wife, Bertie, in 2002.

Music has always been important to Emerson, who had started playing guitar at the age of 14. He even had his guitar with him during his military training in the States.

Later in life, at the age of 57, he took up a banjo and mandolin and added that to his repertoire of instruments. Emerson and Bertie enjoy playing in a bluegrass Gospel band. They perform at churches and nursing homes.

It's been a life filled with many miles and many tunes for Emerson. Looking back over it all he reflected, "The Lord had been good to me. He gave me a good wife (Ruby) and then he gave me another one (Bertie)." Emerson remains thankful for his many blessings!

Kermit and Bertie.

Kermit and his grandchildren.

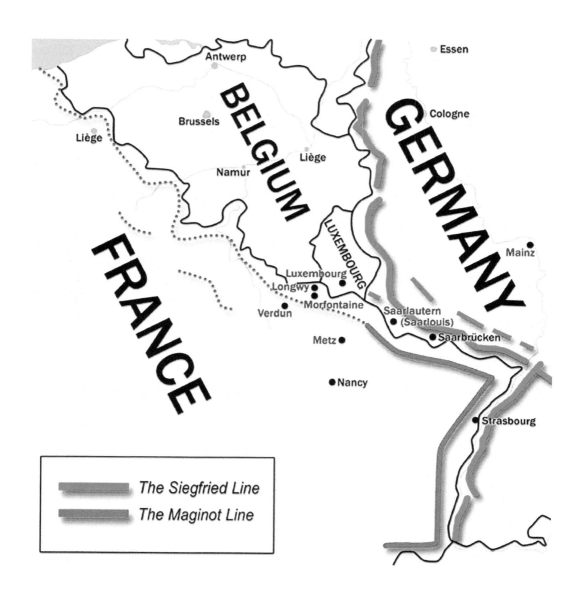

American soldiers cross the Siegfried Line and march into Germany, 1944.

Life on the Big Guns
Veteran Served as Artilleryman in World War II

There were many big guns in use during World War II. Some were mounted on ships and some were on planes. But many were pulled along the ground and used by the infantry. John Jackson of Martinsville, Indiana knows a thing or two about one of those big guns. He spent seven months in combat during World War II on a howitzer gun crew.

Jackson was born on March 12, 1922 in Baker Township near Martinsville, Indiana. He was the oldest of three children raised by his parents, Virgil and Cecil Jackson.

After graduating from Paragon High School in 1940, Jackson worked at Stuart Warner in Indianapolis. He was drafted into the Army in December of 1942.

Following his basic training at Camp Maxey in Texas he reported to the Louisiana Maneuver Area and then completed advanced training in Texas at Camp Swift.

He was trained as an artilleryman and assigned to the 379th Field Artillery Battalion, which was part of the 102nd 'Ozark' Infantry Division.

The division reported to Fort Dix, New Jersey in August of 1944 and began their trek to Europe in September.

105 mm gun crew, with Jackson in center.

Following a two week crossing of the Atlantic Ocean, they landed at Cherbourg, France. After hauling supplies to Paris, the division proceeded to the border of Holland and Germany and entered into combat.

For the next seven months (October 1944–May, 1945) the division battled German forces along the Siegfried line and slowly pushed its way into Germany.

Crew preparing to fire 105 mm.

Jackson was assigned to a gun section on the 105 mm Howitzer. Classified as a light howitzer (there were much bigger ones, like the 240 mm giant), it had a relatively short barrel and was more easily transported than some of the heavier guns. It could fire a projectile up to 8,000 yards down range to support the advancing infantry.

Each howitzer had eight or nine men that served as the crew. Some were responsible for loading the 95-pound projectiles into the barrel. Other men had the duty of adding the correct charges to ignite the projectile. And others helped with setting the sights, aiming and firing the weapon. The men were trained in each task and would rotate in their assigned duties.

When fired, the howitzer would produce a thunderous boom and the breach of the cannon would jerk backwards violently, threatening to injure or kill anyone who mistakenly stood directly behind it.

Although the guns were usually set back a mile from the front lines of combat, the guns and her crews were frequent targets for German Luftwaffe planes and enemy artillery rounds.

"German planes were flying over us all the time", remarked Jackson. "But our big worry was the 88's (German anti-aircraft cannon)," he said. "We'd hear them coming through the air and we'd jump into our foxholes!" He added with sadness, "They got some of our men."

Foxholes were always the first order of business whenever the gun crew moved their howitzer to a new location. "The first thing you did was dig foxholes and pile the dirt around the guns," Jackson said. "Then we put camouflage netting over the gun."

It took most of the winter for the 102nd Division to slowly move through the Siegfried line (a 390 mile long defensive line of bunkers, pillboxes and tank traps built by the Germans to halt enemy advances into Germany).

The dragon teeth obstacles made it difficult for vehicles and equipment to move across, but the 102nd Division and other Allied forces did cross it and made it as far as the Elbe River, 50 miles from Berlin. They stopped there while the Russian forces from the East advanced into Berlin. With their country surrounded, Germany surrendered on May 7th, 1945.

"Every May 7th — that's my best day", said Jackson. "That was the day it was finally over."

Jackson recalled the spectacle of seeing hundreds of German troops crossing the Elbe River and surrendering to the Allied forces. Most of them preferred to surrender to the Americans or British rather than the Russians.

Jackson also remembered seeing large stockpiles of German weapons collected from the surrendering troops.

At war's end Jackson and many others from his division were assigned occupation duty in Germany. For seven months he and the men of his unit provided a show of force throughout Germany. "We'd be in one part for a while, and then they would move us to another part," he recalled. "I was all over Germany and went as far south as the Austrian border."

Germans after surrender.

Stockpile of German weapons.

One day Jackson had the opportunity to visit "the Eagle's Nest," Hitler's mountain hideout in Berchtesgaden, located in southeastern Germany near the Austrian and Czech border.

There was an underground elevator that took people from the parking area up to the peak where the building was located. But using the elevator was a privilege reserved for the few. A sign nearby read, "For Field Grade Officers Only".

**Entrance to elevator at Hitler Hideout, left. Soldiers hold sign from hideout, top right.
Jackson outside Hitler's Hideout, bottom right.**

It just so happened that on the day Jackson was there General Eisenhower was also visiting the hideout. When Eisenhower saw the sign he removed the restriction and said that everyone could ride the elevator. "So, I got to ride the elevator," said Jackson.

He had another treat while in Germany. One day Jackson met up with his brother, Loren, who was serving in the Army Air Forces.

Jackson finally left Germany and returned to the United States in the spring of 1946.

He worked for Collier Brothers Creamery in Martinsville for a few years.

In May of 1947, he married Mary Grace Baker, whom he had met at a carnival in Martinsville when he was home on furlough in 1944. From 1948 through 1963 the couple welcomed the births of five children: three sons and two daughters.

Jackson today, holding two German "souvenirs" from the war.

Jackson found work as a control board operator at the IPL power station north of Martinsville. He worked there for the next 32 years, retiring in 1984.

Toward the end of his career at IPL, Jackson began to raise cattle on his parents' farmland. For 20 years he cut hay, fed the cattle and enjoyed the beef. He even sold some of it to his coworkers.

Today the Jackson clan includes nine grandchildren and six great-grandchildren. But the clan is also minus one of Jackson's sons who died in 1988 at the age of 24 from Hodgkins disease.

The one-time artilleryman continues to live with his wife, Mary in the home they have shared for the last 50 years. The couple celebrated their 65th wedding anniversary in 2012. And, on most mornings, you will find them gathering for conversation and coffee with friends at McDonalds.

Long and Difficult Journey Home

Veteran Endures Combat in Europe and Long Recovery from Injuries

The men who fought in World War II had long journeys back home after the war's end. Maurice Kent of Martinsville, Indiana had a longer journey than most.

Injured during the Battle of the Bulge, Kent's journey included a five-month stay at a hospital in England followed by two years of hospitalization in the states. But eventually, with some determination and luck, he finally made his way back home and to his former life.

Kent, who was the second oldest of five children from Edward Kent and Gail Rutan, was born on June 27, 1922. After the death of his mother when he was just 7 years old, Kent was raised in Morgan County by his maternal grandparents. He attended Buffalo and North schools through the 8th grade.

Kent has fond memories of taking trips into Martinsville with his grandmother on Saturday mornings. "Oh, it was a real treat to come to town with Grandma in the horse and buggy," he said. "We'd park the horse on the north side of the square and walk to places like the JC store and Red's sandwich shop."

As a young boy he was once playing with a friend when he saw a well-dressed man in a suit with a shoulder holster walk into a nearby house. About an hour later, a young girl from inside the house came out and told Kent the man inside wanted him to go through the park and over to the gas filling station to make sure the coast was clear. Kent obliged and returned shortly to give the all clear sign. The well-dressed man handed Kent a ten dollar bill and told him he would be back in a few weeks and would pay him again to be his lookout. Kent served as the man's lookout twice more (collecting $20 in cash) before he found out the man's real identity. "Come to find out, it was John Dillinger," Kent exclaimed!

As he got older Kent worked on the farm owned by the Rutan's for $5.00 a day and dinner. He raised enough money to eventually purchase a Model T Ford.

In 1942 Kent was drafted into the Army. "There were 57 of us drafted from Martinsville," he recalled.

After his basic training at Fort Dix, New Jersey, he was assigned to the 102nd Ozark Division and sent to advanced infantry training in Fort Houston, Texas. On the train ride to Texas he recalled the train coming to a stop somewhere in Missouri. The soldiers were told to get out of the car and guard the tracks. It turned out that President Roosevelt was passing through on a train to California.

During infantry training Kent, who was still only a Private First Class, told the men in his squad, 'I'm going to be your boss someday boys!" They replied, "You don't have enough education for that." Kent retorted, "Boys, where we're going you don't need an education; you need know how. And you don't got it, I know that. But I do!" His prophecy would come true hours before the D-day invasion.

Following his infantry training in Texas, Kent and some other men from the 102nd were assigned to augment the 29th Infantry Division, which had been tasked as one of the first divisions to begin preparing for the Normandy Invasion.

In May of 1943, Kent shipped out to England from the port of New York. "I never saw so many ships in my life," he recalled of the 65 ship convoy that left together. He was in a troop transport with 15,000 men.

Kent arrived in Tidworth Barracks in Devon, England and began training with the 29th Division on the grounds of the Slapton Sands in preparation for the massive amphibious landing planned for Normandy the following year. He was promoted to Corporal and became an assistant squad leader.

The great amphibious invasion of France, code named 'Operation Overlord,' took place on June 6, 1944. Just before Kent's unit disembarked, his Lieutenant came up to him and named him the assistant squad leader. "You hear that boys," Kent said? "What did I tell you in Texas? I'm your boss now."

The 29th Division landed at Omaha Beach, a site of the worst carnage.

"We hit the beach at 6 am," Kent remembered. "They were throwing the lead right on us," he recalled of the German response to the Allied landing. "There were

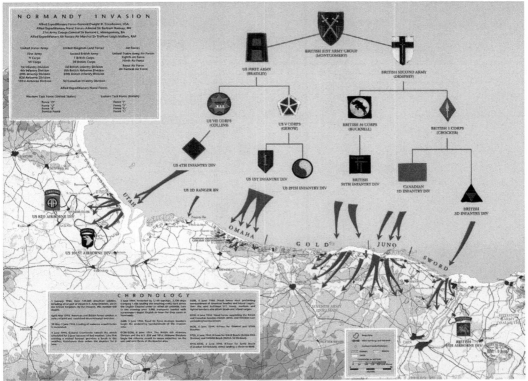

Map of Normandy.

200 Jerries (a slang term referring to the Germans) on that mountain when we landed at Normandy," Kent said. "They sent the Rangers in and we lost about 92 of them on that mountain. So finally, they called in the fighter planes and bombers to destroy them."

Unbeknownst to Kent at the time, his mother's youngest brother was killed the same day while landing on Utah beach, just east of where Kent landed at Omaha. Kent's uncle was 21 years old. He was buried at the American cemetery in Normandy.

After getting ashore and securing the bluff tops, the division pushed inland. They discovered that the Germans were heavily dug in under the hedgerows. Instead of pushing their luck, the infantry waited 3 days for Patton's tanks to arrive and provide the necessary firepower to overrun the enemy. "The Jerries came out and surrendered once Patton arrived with the tanks," Kent recalled.

Kent in combat, upper right with pistol drawn.

It wouldn't be the first time that Patton's tanks came to the rescue of the infantry. "Patton saved our bacon two or three times with his 40 tanks. He was mean," Kent said! "But he could sure handle the tanks!"

The division slowly fought its way across Northern France. Kent remembered taking one French town only to lose three of his men to drinking. Some of the men wanted to get some liquor from the tavern in town. Kent tried to discourage them. "Leave it alone boys," he told them. "The Germans know that Americans like their liquor, and they may have poisoned it." Three days later several of the men who ingested the liquor died from the poison.

Along the way there were plenty of challenges. "I saw some awful things over there," Kent said, referring to not only combat but the German prison camps filled with dead Jews. "I often wonder what the Germans did with their hair after gassing them."

He also remembered losing a good friend, Davenport, to enemy fire. "He tried to run through the crossfire and he got killed. He was a good man!"

Kent recalled another combat challenge in Holland when the Germans had his unit pinned down. "We found the Jerries in the windmills," he said. "They had us zeroed in. We had to call on Patton's tanks to chase them out. When the big guns started shooting they came out running and surrendered!"

While in Holland Kent's unit passed through Haarlem; the same town that Corrie ten Boom lived in. "I know where her dad had the watch shop," Kent said.

In spite of the constant danger, Kent never succumbed to fear. "I was different from the other guys," he said. Grabbing a worn New Testament from the table and putting it into his shirt pocket he went on, "I had this with me and read it to the boys. I wasn't afraid, because I had God with me."

Dog eared and stained by dirty finger prints, Kent used his New Testament often during combat and especially during his long recovery from the injury he sustained during the Battle of the Bulge in January of 1945.

He doesn't have any memory of what happened on that day. He recalled being bogged down in his fox hole from the German artillery and tanks. "They were throwing everything they had on us, and we were doing the same," he said.

He recalled thinking that the 88s were getting closer. Next thing he knew, he woke up in a Belgian field hospital with no dog tags, no pack, no .45 pistol and no helmet. The impact from a German 88 shell had exploded, damaging his nose, jaw (he lost most of his teeth), and feet. He wouldn't walk again on his own for over 2 years.

"Nurse, how long have I been here," he asked?

"Five days," she replied. "You are leaving tonight for England on a C-47."

He's not sure what happened to the buddy that was in the fox hole with him. He never saw or heard from him again.

Kent was transported to the 187th General Hospital in London, where he spent the next five months of initial convalescence from January to May of 1945.

That first morning in the hospital a group of eight nurses on patient bathing detail came forward with their scrubbing brushes and buckets of water, creating quite a stir among the injured men in that ward! Kent recalled, "I hadn't had a bath since I got out of the ocean (the previous June's invasion landing) and had slept on the ground and laid in the mud and snow and ice."

In June of 1945 he returned to the States, but he didn't make it home. He was admitted to the hospital at Camp Butler in North Carolina, where he spent the next 12 months continuing to heal from his wounds. He also began the painful task of rehabilitation.

At the end of twelve months, he got a short 30 day leave to go home for the first time since leaving for the war. It was on this leave that he met and started dating his future wife, Elnora 'Jean' Northern. Kent had just come off the bus in Martinsville when he approached Jean and her friend. "What's going on, girls," he said? "Surely something is going on. I'm home for 30 days, and I have 700 dollars in my pocket that I want to spend." Jean and her girlfriend were willing partners in the spending spree. The three went to a picnic in Quincy, Indiana where Kent purchased some hats for them and had a photograph taken of them.

Kent and Jean, 1945.

His love for Jean had begun.

He'd actually met Jean as a young boy when he was staying at his grandparents. "I threw pebbles at her when she was riding her tricycle," he said sheepishly. "She went running inside the house crying and her mother came out. I ran away." Kent figured he was seven at the time and Jean was three. "I don't' know why, but I never told her I was the boy who threw the pebbles at her," he said laughing.

Following his visit home, he had to return to the hospital in North Carolina for another 12 months of rehabilitation. He and Jean stayed in touch, writing frequently during that year apart.

When he finally returned home for good in 1947, he and Jean married and began their lives together. Their marriage was blessed with five children: Michael, Max, Mark, Rhonda and Debbie. Three of Kent's sons went on to serve in the Army, just as their father had done.

Amtrak, Beech Grove, 1980.

Maurice in Washington, DC on an Indy Honor Flight to see the memorial erected in his honor.

Kent found work initially spray painting farm equipment. He later landed a job at the railroad in Beech Grove, a place he would work for the next forty years. He started out at $.86 cents an hour working on steam engines and later went into the freight shop. His work involved both cutting down cars with a blow torch and nailing up lining in the boxcars or installing passenger doors. Kent retired from the railroad in the late 1980s.

Maurice holding the New Testament he kept with him during combat, and a sign detailing his service to our country.

In 1953, while still working at Amtrak, Kent began painting area houses for side jobs at $.65 an hour. It was a job that he continued for the next 35 years, finally giving up the paint brush in 1988.

His beloved, Jean, died in 2008; but not before they celebrated 60 years of marriage together.

Kent remains active. He turned 92 in 2014. He continues to attend church regularly, something that he has done all of his life. And, in April of 2014, he traveled to Washington, DC on an Indy Honor Flight to see the memorial erected in his honor. A hero's welcome awaited him when he got back to the airport!

Getting back from the war was a long journey for Kent. But he has made the most of the opportunity to return from a war that claimed so many lives. And he has lived his life to the fullest.

Loading Bombs throughout Europe
Armorer Supports War Effort from the Underbelly of B-26 Marauders

Some men fly the planes that drop the bombs in combat. Other men load the planes with the bombs that are going to be dropped. The war effort required both types of men. Carl Marsh of Indianapolis was a bomb loader.

Born August 7, 1923, Marsh, as a young boy, developed a mechanical interest in how things worked — like cars and planes. He graduated from Tech High School in the mechanical program in 1942, just 6 months following the Japanese attack on Pearl Harbor. Wanting to serve his country but not wanting to be drafted into the Army Infantry, Marsh decided to enlist in the U.S. Army Air Forces.

Marsh spent the first 6 months of 1943 undergoing various phases of military training, starting with Basic Training at MacDill Field in Tampa, Florida. Because of his poor eyesight, he was not a candidate for becoming a pilot or bombardier, but he was a good candidate for becoming an Armorer & Mechanic.

Following his basic training, Marsh was sent to the Air Corps/Army Air Forces Technical Training Command located at Lowry Field in Denver, CO for a 9-week course in Armament Maintenance. Combat planes had an array of complicated and lethal machinery (machine guns, canon, bombs, gun turrets, bombsights, etc.) that exceeded the skill set of plane mechanics and required specialized knowledge and training.

B-26 Marauder.

Upon his return to MacDill Field in FL, Marsh was assigned to the 584th Squadron of the 394th Bomb Group, which had officially been activated on March 5, 1943. This was a medium bomb group providing support for the Martin B-26 Marauder.

The Marauder was a twin-engine medium bomber built by Glen L. Martin Company. It held a crew of 6 men and could carry a maximum bomb load of 4000 lbs. The B-26 became a much-used and celebrated workhorse for medium bombing missions in Europe.

In July of 1943, the 584th Squadron left MacDill Air Field for Ardmore Army Airfield in Ardmore, OK for additional training.

Carl, left, and John Corostil working in England, 1944.

As 1944 began, preparations for movement to the European Theater were in full gear for the 584th Squadron. Flight crews left with their aircraft for the trip to England in late January. From February 1-14 the ground echelon packed all the squadron equipment for the trip overseas. The remainder of the squadron then boarded a train and departed for Camp Miles Standish, located in Taunton, MA ~ some 900 miles away. On the 27th of February the troops moved to the Boston Port of Embarkation. Late that night they were all loaded on to a U.S. Army Transport Ship named the George W. Goethals. And, at 0330 on 28 February, the ship, in a convoy with other ships, departed for an unknown destination.

On March 9th the men disembarked at Greenock, Scotland, boarded a train and traveled all night. When they awoke on March 10th, they found themselves in Essex, England (30 miles northeast of London) at their first overseas duty station — the Royal Air Force Station at Boreham Field.

Thirteen days after arriving in England, the 584th Squadron completed their first combat mission of dropping bombs at German locations in France.

Carl with bombs in England.

Marsh and the other members of the ground echelon settled into the routine of checking and loading medium bombs into the B-26 Marauders and performing necessary maintenance on the sophisticated equipment. They soon also settled into another routine — taking cover during the frequent German air raids. Before long, taking cover was just a normal part of everyday life.

The 584th Squadron remained at Boreham Air Field in Essex, England for the next four months.

When the men were awakened from sleep at 0100 on June 6, 1944 and told to gather for a 0215 brief, Marsh and his comrades knew the massive invasion of France had been scheduled for that day. The squadron's mission was to knock out the German's heavy coastal guns along the Normandy coast just before the arrival of the landing force.

At 0300 the B-26 Marauders left England with a host of other aircraft to begin their critical mission. Marsh and the other members of the ground crew worked steadily at loading the 250 lb bombs (each man had to lift 120 lbs. each) on the Marauders for 38 straight hours without food or sleep! It was exhausting.

Ground crew loading bombs.

Squadron eating in the field.

By the end of the mission, 300 B-26 planes had dropped over 13,000 bombs on German defenses in the Normandy landing sector. Although thousands of forces would be killed in the initial landing, thousands more were spared death because of the work of the 584th Squadron at taking out many of the German defenses.

At the end of June, the 584th Squadron had completed 26 vital missions in support of the Allied landing into France. On July 27th the squadron relocated to Holmsley South Field in the southern part of England so that the squadron could give closer air support to the ground forces in France.

The squadron moved again at the end of August — this time across the English

Field bathroom facility.

Channel to the Tour-en-Bessin Airfield in France known as A-13, located near the city of Bayeux in Normandy. This marked the first time that the squadron was in occupied territory and the first time that they lived in full field conditions. The move was necessary in order for the squadron to keep within close air support range

Barracks, Cambrai, France.

Carl, kneeling right, and buddies outside barracks at Cambrai.

of the ever-advancing Allied forces across France. Troop morale dropped a bit during this time frame due to an abundance of rain and a delay of mail delivery from home.

After a brief stay at the Bricy Air Field at the end of September, the squadron relocated again — this time to the northwest area of Cambrai-Niergnies to an airfield known as A74. The airfield had earlier been in German hands and used by the Luftwaffe. Ironically, the 394th Bomb Group had bombed the same airfield in May when it was operating out of Boreham in England.

On October 10th the squadron settled in the small village of Seranvillers, which was 3 miles south of the city of Cambrai and only 25 miles from the Belgian border. With so many moves, the squadron had begun to think that their nickname should be "move a month" squadron. But Cambrai would become their base for operations and their home for the next seven months — their longest stay at any European airfield.

As it slowly dawned on the men that they would be staying in Cambrai for a while, they got to work making a more comfortable and enjoyable living quarters. The squadron had the good fortune to be quartered in buildings used as barracks.

The war-tempo picked up considerably in the month of December as the Germans broke through the Allied lines at St. Vith. Air raid alerts also increased. During one such late night air raid, Marsh showed up at the bunker in his underwear. Cold and tired of waiting for the all-clear signal, he turned back toward the barracks and called out in defiance: "They can kill me inside where it is warmer." And he promptly went back inside.

Carl in his skivvies.

Christmas Day did not bring an end to the flying missions. Two were flown on this day because, after a stretch of bad weather, a window of favorable weather dawned on Christmas morning. Following the completion of their flight missions the squadron enjoyed a wonderful Christmas diner of turkey with all the trimmings. There was also a party in the mess hall for the French children of Seranvillers. The men had donated some of the food articles they had received from home and put them into gift bags so that each child could enjoy a real Christmas present. The presents were given to the kids in front of the large Christmas tree in the mess hall. Christmas songs were then sung by everyone.

The peace and tranquility of a Christmas celebration was short lived, however. Ten days before Christmas of 1944, the Germans, who had successfully concealed their troop movement toward the Allied front lines in Belgium, suddenly began a counter-offensive attack in the Ardennes forest designed to split the Allied forces. From December 16-25, the Germans advanced far enough

Barracks on Christmas day 1944, Cambrai, France.

Marsh, second from left, and men passing under trees.

westward to create a "bulge" in the weakened Allied lines in Belgium, France and Luxembourg — thus the familiar title for this conflict was the "Battle of the Bulge".

The 584th Squadron's missions were directed in support of the Allied effort to push back the Germans and regain control of Belgium. Weather, which had been poor for much of December, cleared and became more favorable for flying in late December. For the next several weeks the squadron worked hard in bitterly cold weather to keep flight operations going in support of the front line fighting. With the extremely low temperatures weapons had to be routinely maintained and vehicle engines run every half hour or so to prevent their oil from congealing. Marsh recalled being bitterly cold and sleeping with all his clothes on each night in the barracks.

There continued to be much snow and colder than normal temperatures throughout January of 1945. The ground echelon of the squadron, when not servicing planes and loading bombs, kept busy clearing taxi strips for the planes to take off and land.

Bombs waiting to be loaded.

The weather started to improve in February. Of the 23 missions flown, the majority of them were supply and marshaling areas directly ahead of the Allied Armies as they began their advance into German territory. February was the first month that the group began dropping propaganda leaflets in German towns informing the inhabitants of the Allies progress.

On April 12th, the squadron learned of the death of President Roosevelt. The news shocked them all. A time of mourning ensued. The squadron paid tribute to the President during a group memorial revue held on the following Sunday.

The 271st and final mission for the bomb squadron was on April 20th. It was a leaflet drop in Germany. Of significant note, there was no flak experienced on any of the missions, indicating that Hitler's forces were weakened and on the run.

As news of Germany's May 7th unconditional surrender reached the 584th Squadron it was in the middle of another move — this one further east to Venlo, Holland to a huge airfield called Y55, most of which was on German soil. The 394th Bomb Group had been assigned as part of the Army of Occupation. The squadron had to set up in tents due to the Germans having bombed all of the buildings before they left. Their occupation duty lasted until August, when they were finally cleared to return home.

One of Marsh's memories during his time near Venlo, Holland was seeing a poor family and coming to their aid. Carl and some friends had walked into town one day when it started to rain. They saw a house with a porch and went under it to wait out the storm. A woman came to the door with some little kids. She asked them to come into her home. Marsh was touched by the site of the young children in their impoverished condition. He noticed a bowl of mashed potatoes on the kitchen table. It was probably all they had to eat. When Marsh got back to the airfield he got some friends together and went to the acquisition officer. They convinced the officer to donate some food to the poor family. Marsh and his buddies went back to the house and left some sacks of food on the porch.

In August 1945, the 394th Bomb Group made their final move. They left the airfield at Venlo, Holland and proceeded to Kitzingen Airfield (R6) in Germany.

Five months later, in February of 1946, the 394th Bomb Group was deactivated and the remaining B-26 Aircraft were stripped and destroyed. In combat summary, the 394th had flown 271 missions with over 9,000 aircraft sorties and over 13,000 tons of explosives dropped. The group had 344 casualties with 182 killed in action, 36 killed in accidents, 59 taken as POWs and 41 wounded in action. A total of 26

Was ist zu tun?

EINZELNE SOLDATEN ODER KLEINE GRUPPEN ergeben sich indem sie Waffen, Helm und Koppel ablegen, die Hände hochheben und entweder ein Taschentuch oder ein Flugblatt schwenken. Sind alliierte Soldaten in unmittelbarer Nähe, so sind diese mit „EI SÖRRENDER" anzurufen. Passierscheine, wenngleich nützlich, sind nicht unbedingt erforderlich. Sammelplätze für Kriegsgefangene befinden sich entlang den Haupt- und Durchgangsstrassen.

Sofern die Übergabe in grösseren Gruppen erfolgt, hat sie unter Beachtung militärischer Disziplin durchgeführt zu werden. Der jeweils befehlshabende Unteroffizier ist verantwortlich für die ordnungsgemässe Durchführung. Offiziere übergeben ihre Einheiten geschlossen, wenn möglich an einen alliierten Offizier gleichen Ranges. Sind Besprechungen erforderlich, so können sich laut Haager Konvention beglaubigte Parlamentäre mit dem nächstgelegenen alliierten Gefechtsstand in persönlicher Verbindung setzen.

BEHANDLUNG VON KRIEGSGEFANGENEN

1. SOFORTIGE ENTFERNUNG aus der Kampfzone. Stammlager stehen für Euch schon bereit.

2. ANSTÄNDIGE BEHANDLUNG. Auf Grund der Genfer Konvention werdet Ihr wie Soldaten behandelt.

3. GUTE VERPFLEGUNG. Ihr erhaltet dieselbe Kost wie wir, das bestverpflegte Heer der Welt.

4. LAZARETTBEHANDLUNG. Eure Verwundeten und Kranken werden genau so behandelt wie die unsrigen.

5. SCHREIBGELEGENHEIT. Ihr könnt je Mann 4 Karten und 4 Briefe per Monat nach Hause schreiben.

6. RÜCKKEHR. Nach Kriegsende werdet Ihr so bald wie möglich nach Hause zurückgeschickt.

ZG 112 K

Männern, deren Altersklasse zu hoch oder zu niedrig ist für wirklichen Frontdienst, Männern, die vor 6 Monaten nur g.v.H. geschrieben waren, einem hohen Prozentsatz von Volksdeutschen und aus unzuverlässigen fremden Einheiten.

Was unter der Besatzung des Walls an kampferprobten Einheiten zu finden ist, soll als Versteifung dienen und dann mit dem Rest geopfert werden.

VON VORNE ANGEGRIFFEN — VON HINTEN ABGESCHRIEBEN

Das ist die Lage am Atlantikwall.

Und das ist nur der Anfang des Zweifrontenkriegs.

Polnisch sprechende Wehrmachtangehörige

Odezwa Armij Sprzymierzonych

POLACY!

1. Wcielono was gwałtem do armji niemieckiej. Najeźdźca napiętnował was hańbiącym mianem Volksdeutscha.

2. Odwieczny wróg Polski rzucił was na ten pas wybrzeża bez rezerw i transportu. Uczynił z was żywe miny, wysunięte przed niemiecką siłą pancerną.

3. Żołnierze, marynarze i lotnicy Narodów Zjednoczonych ruszyli do potężnego szturmu przeciw hitlerowskim Niemcom, — do szturmu, który na zawsze złamie tyranię wspólnego wroga i położy kres niewoli Polaków.

4. Każdy strzał, wymierzony przez was w tych bojowników wolności, byłby strzałem w serce Polski.

5. Każdy Polak, który zaprzestanie bezcelowej walki, zachowa swe życie dla siebie i dla Polski.

POKAŻCIE TĘ ULOTKĘ NASZYM ŻOŁNIERZOM

ZGI

Two of the many flyers dropped by the 394th. The translation for the headline on left is, What is to be done? The second flyer, in both German and Polish, sends two different messages. In German, one portion says, "From the front attacked, from behind forgotten." A portion of the Polish section appeals to their love of country, saying, "Each Pole, who will cease aimless war, will maintain life for Poland."

aircraft (the irony of the number was not lost for a B-26 squadron) were lost in combat.

Their aircraft now replaced, the members of the 584th Squadron slowly began to return home in the late fall of 1945. When his discharge came through Marsh was in the region of the French Riviera in southeastern France, near the Mediterranean coastline, waiting for further instructions on where to report next. He had volunteered to be sent to the South Pacific in support of the Allied invasion of Japan. When the Japanese surrendered after the atomic bomb drops on their homeland, there was no need for further Army Air Force Squadron support. So, Marsh finally returned home in November of 1945.

Carl and Pat.

When Marsh returned from the war, he began dating Rosemarie (Pat) Curtis of Indianapolis. He married her on August 10, 1952. God blessed their marriage with three children: Curt, Carla and Rosie. Later, their family grew by two spouses and four grandchildren. Marsh and Pat went on to enjoy 59 years of marriage.

Marsh went from working on planes to working on cars after he returned home. He opened Marsh Garage on May 5, 1958 in Indianapolis. When Marsh opened, his father Henry, who had been a mechanic since he was a teenager, began working with him. In 1970 the garage building across the street became available and Marsh bought it and expanded the business.

Marsh retired in 1988 and the day to day operation of the service garage was turned over to his son Curt, who had been working there full time since 1973. Marsh returned to repairing vehicles in 1995 and continued to work until June of 1997.

Marsh built some lifelong friendships with some of the guys from the 584th Squadron. The men all scattered when they returned home from the war. However,

Carl (far right) next to his father, working at Marsh Garage.

many of them kept in touch with letters and Christmas cards. In 1987, as Marsh was recovering from surgery and couldn't work at the garage, he decided to take a trip to Ohio to visit Don Carper, one of his friend's from the squadron. What followed after that visit was the start of annual squadron reunions — many of which Marsh and his wife, Pat organized and hosted. The reunions began in 1988 and continued through 2004.

Carl, third from right in second row, at one of the 584th Squadron reunions.

The friends in his squadron were never far from Marsh's thoughts. Every time he went down to the basement in his home he passed by a large unit reunion photo hanging from a wall in the stairway. He never failed to pause and tap the photo gently as he passed by it. The men of the 584th Squadron were, after all these years, still his brothers in arms and his comrades for life.

Marsh was active in his community and his church. He was also a member of the Board of Directors at Camp Lakeview (a Lutheran Camp in Southern Indiana) and was a member of the Lutheran Service Club. He also enjoyed woodworking, spending time with family and relaxing at their lake cottage on Lutheran Lake.

After 89 years of life, God called Carl Marsh home to heaven on January 5th, 2012. His faithful and loving wife, Pat kept her promise to him and cared for him in his home until his death.

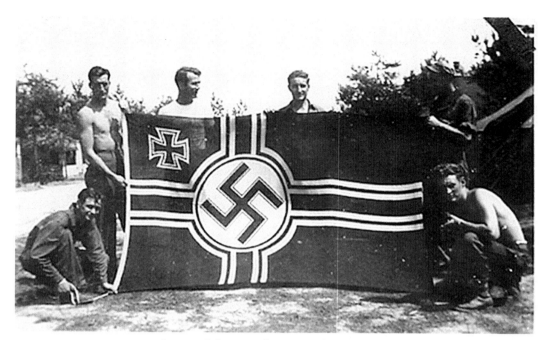

Captured German Flag in Cambrai, France.

Top L-R: William L Adams, 1Lt Gordon R Carlstrand, 1Lt Charles C Garrett, Donald Videtto.
Bottom L-R: SSgt Corben E Allen, 1Lt Arthur S Bartlett — 394th BS.

From Throwing Balls to Dropping Bombs
World War II Changes Life's Course for Chicago Native

As a young boy, Paul Maves wanted to become a baseball star. The Lyons, Illinois (west suburb of Chicago) native grew up loving the game and rooting for his hometown team, the Chicago White Sox. "I went to my first ball game in 1930 as a second grader," he recalled. "My father took me. I'll never forget walking up to Sox Park and seeing this green grass in the infield. It was amazing!"

But World War II changed the pursuit of baseball for Maves. In fact, it changed everything for him!

After graduating from high school in Cicero, Illinois in June of 1941, Maves worked briefly at the International Harvester Plant in Chicago. When Pearl Harbor was attacked six months later, he knew that his life was about to change.

"I knew the draft was catching up to me," said Maves. "I saw Jimmy Cagney and Pat O'Brien in the old World War I movies. They were in the trenches and the bullets were flying and I thought, That's not for me! I'm going to get in the Air Force so that when you come back from the mission you've got a nice bed to sleep in and warm meals to eat."

TRAINING

Maves enlisted in the Army Air Forces in October of 1942 and was sent to Miami, Florida to complete his basic training. Following a brief stay at the University of Toledo for his College Training Detachment, Maves went to Nashville, Tennessee for his Classification Training. This was where the Army Air Force determined whether Maves would train as a pilot, bombardier or navigator.

He was initially disqualified for bombardier training because he was left-handed. Bombardiers had to learn to use the Norden Bomb Sight, which could only be operated by the right hand. However, during the initial reaction test that all the cadets had to take, the instructors discovered that Maves was quite adept at using his right hand. Because of his right-hand proficiency, the instructors made an exception and directed Maves to begin training as a bombardier.

During the next several months, Maves attended Pre-Flight School, Gunnery School, and finally Bombardier School. By March of 1944, with 14 months of training behind him, he was finally ready to be assigned to a plane and crew.

ASSIGNMENT TO THE B-26 MARAUDER

Initially assigned to the B-17 plane, Maves saw a notice advertising the need for bombardiers on the B-26 bomber and decided to sign up. He spent April and May of 1944 in Shreveport, Louisiana training on the B-26, Martin Marauder. The

B-26 in flight.

Marauder, a twin-engine medium bomber built by Glen L. Martin Company, carried a crew of seven: pilot, co-pilot, bombardier, navigator, mid upper gunner and tail gunner. She could be airborne for 1,100 miles (6 hours) and could carry a bomb load of up to 4,000 pounds. Her defense armament consisted of 11 M2 50 caliber machine guns.

B-26s in formation.

The aircraft, however, was a dangerous one. It's propensity for accidents in training led to a common phrase at Barksdale Army Air Field, *"One a day in the Bay."* In spite of such initial high losses, the B-26 became a much-used and celebrated workhorse for medium bombing missions in Europe.

OFF TO EUROPE

By September, 1944, following the completion of their B-26 training, Maves and his crew picked up the B-26 assigned to them and departed Bangor, Maine for Europe. Lifting off from the airfield with their fully loaded B-26 proved to be a "close-call." Maves recalled: "They said to me, 'Maybe you ought to be in the nose of the plane for takeoff.' They didn't usually do that. But the plane was so loaded with equipment that there was hardly room for all the crew. So we took off. We were climbing very, very slowly. And all of a sudden I looked out and here come the pine trees ahead of us. And I thought, *Oh my God, I'm going to be goosed and killed by the pine trees!* We just barely cleared them, and that was the last time I ever took off in the nose of the plane!"

Following their safe flight across the Atlantic Ocean, the crew reported for duty to Matching Green, England, which was the base for the Allied Air Forces. It was here that the crew was assigned to the 572nd Squadron in the 391st Bomb Group of the 9th Air Force Division.

MEMORABLE FLIGHT MISSIONS:

Bombardier Duties: As the bombardier, Maves was assigned to the tight space located in the nose of the aircraft. The space was surrounded by windows so that he could get a good view of things in front and beneath him. A 50-caliber machine gun could be set up in the nose when it was necessary for additional frontal shooting.

The bombardier's main mission was to drop the plane's bomb load on the designated targets. Each bombardier in the squadron took his cue for the bomb drops by watching the lead plane in the formation through the nose window. "When he dropped, we dropped," said Maves. "The lead bombardier always aimed short so that if he was past the target the rest of the bombs wouldn't be. We would see the bombs hit and pretty much know if we hit the target." Although smoke from the first detonated bombs would sometimes prevent a clear view of impact.

Dropping the bombs consisted of two switches: one to open the door and one to drop the bombs. B-26 aircraft carried 2,000 pounds of bombs at the most. After

B-26 bomb bay.

each bombardier released his bomb load, he would inform the pilot it was ok to turn with the words: "Bombs away! OK to turn." The pilot would then turn up and away to get past the impact area.

The First Mission: Maves' first combat flight mission came on September 29th of 1944. It was to be his crew's only mission leaving from the airfield at Matching Green, England. And it was also the only mission in which the crew didn't make it back to the airfield on the same day it had left. The crew had to land in Brussels following their bomb run because they didn't have enough fuel to make it all the way back to England. The rest of their missions would be flown out of the Army Airfield at Roye-Amy, France, which the squadron relocated to shortly after Maves arrived in England.

Missions in General: Missions were flown in sections of six planes. Bombing targets included: bridges, railroad yards, supply depots, ammunition dumps —

B-26 Marauder taking off.

anything that would deter the Germans from getting more troops or supplies up to the front lines. "We went directly behind the lines for our bombings," said Maves, "whereas the heavy's (heavy bombers) went further inland to the factories."

The crews were instructed not to come back with any of their bomb load. Maves remembered, "We always laughed at that. At the end of the month they published a report on how many tons of bombs were dropped on Germany. Well (laughing), they were on Germany all right; but not necessarily on the target."

After returning from each mission, the crews would debrief, and everyone would share their observations about the mission and note any corrections that might be useful for future missions.

The Close-Call Mission: The crew was over Germany when their engine started acting up. Unable to hold their altitude at 11,000 feet, they were forced to descend to a much lower and more dangerous altitude. With one engine out, they were unable to keep up with the other planes in their squadron and were soon out of sight and all alone in enemy territory. It had been an afternoon flight, so eve-

B-26 Marauder bombing Germany.

ning was approaching. As twilight descended Maves saw flashes from the ground as German artillery starting shooting at them. Following each flash of light Maves, remembering his training on how long it took for an 88 millimeter projectile (the infamous German anti-aircraft artillery guns) to reach a certain elevation, used his watch to count to ten and then instructed the pilot to turn so that the plane moved away from the path of the airborne projectile. Maves kept watching the flashes, counting the seconds and directing the turns until they got out of enemy range. The crew finally guided the hobbled plane safely back to their airfield in France.

The next day, after inspecting the plane, the crew chief informed Maves' crew that there were about 300 small holes all around the plane and one of them, likely from the big "German 88" was a 3 inch hole right through the wing that was very close to the gas tanks in the wings. Had it struck the gas tanks, the plane would have certainly gone down and the crew likely killed. "We really should have gotten written up (for a medal) for getting that plane back," said Maves. "But we never did."

Although he did not experience fear very often, Maves admitted to this being the mission that caused him the most concern. But even concern couldn't remove the thrill of the contest from him during the threatening 'cat and mouse' game. Ever the competitive athlete, he enjoyed the duel between him and the guy firing the gun on the ground. "I was competing with the guy down there," he said, referring to the enemy artillerymen. "He was trying to outwit me and I was trying to outwit him. *Missed me that time!* It was a challenge of my judgment against the guy on the ground. I hate to say this, but it was a game, a lousy game, and a risky game. But I enjoyed it."

The Group Mission: On one occasion Maves' bomb group was behind the lead group. The lead group had already entered the IP (initial point) and, as they turned out from dropping their bombs, they were being shot down by the flak of enemy fire. Maves recalled: "The Bombardier's job was to count how many planes were shot down and how many people ejected. But then you know we had to make that turn next. When you are on the bomb run you aren't doing anything but following the group ahead of you. You are using no evasive measures. So you know you are going to enter the same area where the other group had planes being shot down. That one worried me a little."

Fortunately, the planes in Maves' group all made it back safely from that mission.

B-26 Marauder shot down.

The Pathfinder Mission: In the winter, when cloud cover made it impossible to see targets through the Norden bombsight, the 391st Bomb Group relied upon the assistance of the 482nd Pathfinder Group. Pathfinder crews flew B-17 or B-24 aircraft equipped with specially modified British radar systems developed by the Royal Air Force. The radar system was used to determine the location of the target for the bomb drops.

The Pathfinder ship led the group of B-26 Squadrons above the clouds and into the sunshine. "It always amazed me how sunny it was up there above the cloud cover", noted Maves. The German 88's would still be firing at the aircraft, but since they were above the clouds Maves couldn't see the flash from the guns to help direct his plane away from the projectiles. The effort to evade being hit by enemy artillery required a different tactic — the use of "'chaff." "As we approached the target, our job was to throw pieces of aluminum out of the plane's window," Maves explained. The cloud of descending aluminum pieces would be picked up by the enemy radar and would make it impossible for them to distinguish between the pieces of aluminum and the actual plane that was trying to get away.

B-26 formation above the clouds.

The danger of Pathfinder missions above cloud-cover wasn't limited to enemy fire. Maves recalled, "The most exciting thing was on the way back to base when the Pathfinder led the B-26 formations down from the clear skies and back into the cloud cover. You were in a group of six planes and were unable to see the other planes near you in the squadron. You just hoped that everyone kept their positions and didn't hit each other during the descent. The Bombardier's role was to call out to the pilots as soon as he saw ground or a church steeple." Once ground appeared, there often wasn't much time to get ready for landing. Fortunately, Maves' crew had safe landings.

SAD DAYS IN EUROPE

Corporal Grigsby's Death: Tragedy occurred on the morning of October 15th, 1944. While the officers were attending their pre-flight mission, the enlisted crew members on Maves' B-26 were at the plane getting things ready. Enlisted men (flight engineer, rear gunner and the A gunner) did not go to the briefings prior to the mission. Only the officers attended. During the pre-flight preparations, Corporal William Grigsby, the flight engineer, was tragically killed when he accidentally backed into the rotating propeller in front of the wings.

Maves' crew was called out of the briefing following the accident. By the time the officers arrived on the scene, Grigsby's body had already been covered with a blanket. He was later buried at Epinal American Cemetery in France.

Corporal Grigsby was married and had just found out that his wife had given birth to their first child. Maves had met Grigsby's wife once in Savannah, GA when the crew picked up their B-26 plane. She was about 7 months pregnant at the time. "I really felt bad for her," he said. "The baby never got to meet her Dad."

Maves wrote his mother and asked her to send the baby girl a dress from the crew. Grigsby's wife later sent Maves a letter that included a photo of the baby wearing the dress that his mother had purchased and sent on behalf of the crew.

Tragedy Before Christmas: Tragedy and sadness struck again, this time on a much wider scale, on Saturday, December 23rd, 1944, during a mission in the Ardennes. The day became known as Black Saturday in 9th Air Force history. On that awful day, 36 B-26 aircraft were lost due to enemy fire. Of those 36 aircraft, 16 were from the 391st Bomb Group! Thankfully, Maves' squadron (572nd) had not been assigned a flight mission for that day.

Aerial of Ardennes.

There was a very subdued Christmas Eve service that evening. The original plans called for a choir of men to lead in singing some of the Christmas carols. But many of those choir members had been killed in the previous day's tragedy, so there was no choir for the service. "It was the saddest and most subdued Christmas Eve service that I had ever attended," remembered Maves.

Maves and the rest of his crew had to put the tragedy behind them quickly as they flew consecutive missions the next three days — December 24, 25, and 26. These missions were all in support of the Ardennes Battle, known as the "Battle of the Bulge." For their outstanding air support from 23-26 December 1944 the 391st Bomb Group was awarded the Distinguished Unit Citation.

END OF WORLD WAR II!

When news came that the war ended on May 7th, Maves was in Venlo, Holland with the 397th Bomb Group. His crew celebrated the wars' end by shooting off their issued 45 pistols from inside their tents. It was the only time they had ever used their pistols since coming to Europe.

By the time the Japanese surrendered in August of 1945, Maves was home in Chicago on leave. He celebrated VJ Day by attending a carnival sponsored by the American

Shirley Pantke Maves.

Legion in Berwyn (a Chicago suburb). He was wearing his uniform. "A little girl came up to me & asked me for my autograph," Maves recalled.

Maves spent his last few weeks in the Army Air Forces going through the discharge process in North Carolina. While waiting for his discharge he explored his college options and decided to enroll at the University of Wisconsin.

Marriage and College: Maves had begun dating Shirley Pantke, who was a member of his church in Lyons. Once he had decided on a college to attend, he also decided to propose to Shirley. Maves recalled: "So I came back home and I told Shirley, "Ok, I'm going to Wisconsin. Do you want to get married and go to Wisconsin?" Shirley said yes. Paul and Shirley were married on January 12, 1946 at Zion Lutheran Church in Lyons.

In March of 1946 Maves began attending the University of Wisconsin in the civil engineer program. He went to classes year round including summers.

Baseball Dream: At the age of 22, Maves decided to take a long shot and pursue his childhood dream of playing baseball. He was a senior at the University of Wisconsin

Maves family photo.

and it was his last chance to pursue his dream. "I had to satisfy myself and try," said Maves. "But I didn't make it. I knew I wasn't going to make it. For crying out loud, I hadn't played ball for years! I had been in the Army Air Corps. We didn't play ball there. But I went out and went as far as I could with the dream."

Career: Following his graduation from the University of Wisconsin, Maves and his wife went to Milwaukee where he worked for the Wisconsin State Highway Department for a year. The young family then returned to Lyons, IL and Maves began work at an engineering firm in Chicago. In 1965 Maves was transferred to Indianapolis to work at Martin Marietta in their sand gravel plants. He worked there until the mid-1970s. His final job as a civil engineer was with Schneider Engineering in Indianapolis. He worked there from the mid-1970s until 1988 when he retired.

Family: Maves enjoyed 57 years of marriage with Shirley before her death in 2003. God blessed their union with three children: Donald (July 2, 1948), David (July 21, 1953) and Diane (February 26, 1955). The Maves family spent most of their years together in Speedway, Indiana where Maves lived for 45 years.

Latter Years: In these latter years, Maves has appreciated the attention grateful citizens have given him and other World War II veterans. In 2012 he was on the inaugural Indy Honor Flight to Washington D.C., where he received many expressions of thanks. And,

Maves on 2012 Honor Flight.

Maves holding a service flag.

Maves, far left, with other veterans at Pacers game.

in November of 2013, he was one of a dozen World War II veterans honored at half-court during an Indiana Pacers Basketball game.

Although he never played professional baseball, Maves has led a fulfilling life. The war, which changed the pursuit of his dreams also enabled him to perform a sacred duty for his country as well as secure an education that has served him well throughout his career.

Wounded High Over Germany
Veteran Recalls His Injury and Long Road to Recovery

By some estimates, the average crewmember of a B-17 bomber during World War II had only a one in four chance of completing his required 25 missions and remaining alive. Verle Maxwell almost didn't make it past his 3rd flight mission!

The Morgan County, Indiana native was hit by flak on February 25, 1944, while flying a mission over Germany. His was a short experience with combat and a long experience with recovery.

Born on September 8, 1923 in rural Martinsville, Indiana, Maxwell was the 2nd of 10 children raised by his parents, Forest and Martha Maxwell.

Following his graduation from Martinsville High School in 1941, he worked at his father's farm and was hired at Indiana Bell Telephone Company.

When his buddies started joining the service following the attack at Pearl Harbor, Maxwell decided to follow suit, enlisting in the Army Air Forces in February of 1942.

He attended basic training in St. Petersburg, Florida, and then proceeded to Buckley Field in Colorado for Aerial Armament School. Slotted for the position as a tail gunner, he next went to Gunnery School in Las Vegas, Nevada; and, on August 9th, he received his wings and diploma.

(Back L-R) T/Sgt Seymour Berman (R)(Int)(5), 2Lt Elmer P. Israelson (B)(Int)(4), 1Lt Quentin J. Gorman (P)(1), 2Lt Raymond Hofmann (CP)(Int)(2), 2Lt Carroll Binder, Jr.(KIA)(N)(3), Verle Maxwell. (Front L-R) Sgt John B. Galloway (WG)(7), Sgt Ollie G. Crenshaw (BT)(Int)(5), Sgt Bob Jensen (TG)(7), Sgt James O. Williams (WG)(KIA)(6), T/Sgt William R. Blakeney, Jr. (E)(Int)(5).

Maxwell was assigned to a B-17 crew in Salt Lake City, Utah. The crew did further training in Ephrata, Washington, before heading to the Air Force Base at Rapid City, South Dakota to await their orders overseas.

The B-17, called the "Flying Fortress," was a four-engine, high flying heavy bomber designed in the 1930s. It was used primarily in the European theater for bombing industrial and military targets in Germany. It became the most widely used bomber in World War II, dropping more bombs than any other U.S. plane.

The crew of a B-17 consisted of 10 people: Pilot, Co-Pilot, Bombardier, Navigator, Engineer, Radio Operator, Assistant Radio Operator, 2 Waist Gunners and a Tail Gunner.

Maxwell's job as tail gunner was to ward off enemy attacks from behind the plane. The tail gunner, as the name implies, sat at the very rear of the plane, just under the tail section. The gunner squeezed into a small compartment that required him

Verle and his squadron.

to kneel and sit back against his legs as he controlled the twin Browning machine guns protruding from the turret.

It was an advantageous position for firing. It was also an advantageous target for the enemy's fire. Tail Gunners were aware that enemy planes approaching from behind would always try to take them out first.

Maxwell and his B-17 crew, along with their squadron, departed the U.S. on December 2nd of 1943 and headed to England. Leaving from Maine, the plane touched down at Iceland before reaching the Royal Air Force base in Molesworth, England. There, the crew continued its training for combat duty.

Tail gunner.

On February 25, 1944, while on just their 3rd flight mission, their B-17 encountered enemy fire while flying over Augsburg, Germany. Maxwell was hit in the chest by flak from the enemy guns.

Ironically, a day earlier, Maxwell and his crew had attended a memorial service for 69 flyers from the squadron that had died recently in combat. Reminders of death's threat were never far for any of them.

Maxwell remembers getting shot. Some of his crew came over to his compartment to drag him to the radio room. The cold temperature there helped to slow his bleeding and keep him alive. Someone gave him a shot of morphine to help with the pain.

As much as they wanted him to get medical attention, his crew could not break the formation or abort their mission. They continued on to their bombing objective while Maxwell fought to stay alive. It would be several hours before the plane would arrive back in England.

When they safely returned to England, Maxwell was transported to the American Station Hospital.

His wounds were significant. Flak had entered under his armpit and traveled across the left side of his chest, just missing his jugular vein.

He spent the next four months in the station hospital, having several surgeries and being treated for the wounds in his shoulder and chest.

As if to underscore the risk of death to the crew, the man who took Maxwell's place as tail gunner on his B-17 was blown from the turret in an explosion of enemy fire that also ripped the tail of the plane off. He was never found.

Verle, front row center, recovering at base hospital.

And a few days after that tragedy, the plane was shot down over Germany. The crew that survived the crash was captured by the Germans and taken as prisoners of war.

Maxwell returned to the U.S. in June of 1944. He continued being treated for his injuries at Mayo General Hospital in Galesburg, Illinois, and was later transferred to the Army Air Forces Convalescent Hospital in Fort Thomas, Kentucky.

He was given short leaves from his long hospital stays but had to keep returning as the medical staff attempted to get his shoulder to heal.

Maxwell finally returned home for good on July 21, 1946. The date of his homecoming was made even more special because it was also his wife Betty's birthday.

Maxwell had met Betty Goss at Liberty Christian Church when they were in junior high. They started holding hands at church and soon became sweethearts. Maxwell, 2 years her senior, gave Betty a small diamond ring on her 15th birthday.

They married on October 9, 1943 when Maxwell came home for a week furlough from his training in South Dakota. Following the wedding, Betty went out to South Dakota to stay with Maxwell until his crew left for Europe.

Betty sent her husband V-mail letters every day. But it was five weeks before she got the first letter from him.

She continued to write him daily as news of his injury reached her and the family.

When Maxwell finally came back to the U.S. Betty visited him routinely at the hospitals in Illinois and Kentucky.

Maxwell's return home in 1946 finally allowed him to begin the next chapter of his life. He worked at a friend's farm machine business in Martins-

Verle, post injury.

Verle and Betty.

Verle and Betty.

ville for a year before landing a job at the Farm Bureau, where he went on to work for the next 30 years.

He and Betty raised two children: Evelyn and Barry. Their expanded family now includes three grandchildren and some great-grandchildren.

Betty Maxwell died on January 26, 2015. Verle joined her in death on April 25, 2015. They had been married for more than 70 years.

The Maxwell family.

A Critical Design
Veteran Serves His Country as Soldier and Civilian

Charles May's military service during World War II wasn't what he had hoped it would be. There were many disappointments. However, after many years, May found his niche as an engineer and made significant contributions to the Department of Defense with a critical design in radar systems technology.

May was the middle of three children born to his parents, Charles Mitchell May and Martha Ann Hawkins, on July 20, 1926 in Elletsville, Indiana. Following his freshman year, his family moved to Spencer, Indiana. May graduated from Spencer High School in 1944.

Taking a deferred enlistment, May entered the Army Air Force as a volunteer cadet in December of 1944. He had wanted to become a pilot. However toward the end of his basic training at Kessler Air Base near Biloxi, Mississippi, May was informed that he would not get his opportunity to fly. Instead, he was assigned for duty as a central fire gunner (CFG) on B-29s.

Although he was disappointed, he took some solace in knowing that he would still be in the air. But the solace was short lived!

His orders were changed quickly and instead of going to Denver for gunner school, May ended up at Aircraft & Engine Maintenance School in Amarillo, Texas. The Army Air Force had slotted him to become a "grease monkey;" a job in which he really had no interest.

Disappointed once again, May fought back bitterness and resentment and chose instead to focus on service. "I enlisted to win a war," he said. "So I studied hard and did well in school."

But the disappointments kept coming. He was denied even the privilege of helping to win the war when Germany surrendered in May of 1945 as May was training at Davis Monahan Field in Arizona.

Following his training, May was assigned to the 343rd Fighter Squadron in Kaufbeuren, Germany (near Bavaria), arriving in November of 1945. Although he loved the scenery — the base was near the glorious Alps, as well as the German people who were very friendly; he could not find fulfillment in his work of cataloging airplane parts.

To make matters worse, while he was at Kaufbeuren, he received some bad news about his girlfriend back home. The two had been writing letters daily. Suddenly, her letters stopped. "I knew something was wrong," May recalled. "Knowing something is wrong half a world away…what a helpless feeling!" May eventually received a letter from a friend who informed him that his high school sweetheart was marrying another man.

May's life took another downward turn when he was transferred to a new base in Giebelstadt, Germany. Gone were the inspiring views of the Alps and the friendly Bavarian people. In their place were bombed out hangars and Germans with more reservation toward the Americans. Recalled May, "The people were not friendly; in fact, they showed some fear of American soldiers. And Giebelstadt was bland, consisting only of flat crop lands. The only trees left were along the road leading to the only intact hangar."

Although he cared little for the location or the job, May did learn much about different jet engines. Recalling his intensive maintenance course on the new P-80 May said, "What interested me was every five hours of flight time a major inspection was due. I mean major! That meant taking the tail section off of the jet airplane. If the tolerances did not meet specifications, the engine had to be replaced."

When the new P-80 jets began to arrive on base there was much excitement. And there was tragedy as well. May remembered, "When the first three jets came within sight there was great excitement and jubilation. The first jet landed, and there was a round of jubilation. The second jet landed without incident, but the third jet was destroyed by Clear Air Turbulence (CAT) while still in the air. It was twenty years before CAT destroyed another commercial jet aircraft, and that was when they started the CAT studies."

P-80s in flight.

After spending nine months in Germany, May's often frustrating military service finally came to an end in August of 1946, as he was discharged from Camp Sheridan, Illinois.

Following his discharge, May enrolled at Purdue University, graduating with a B.A. in Electrical Engineering. After graduating in 1953, he moved to Indianapolis and took a job in the Department of Defense, working specifically for the Navy as a research engineer.

"As a young engineer I was to research what frequencies were suitable for radar systems," May said. "I was involved in all the electromagnetic frequencies including radar, radio, infrared, visual, ultraviolet, x-ray and gamma radiation."

May found much satisfaction in his career! After years of frustration and disappointment on active duty, he had found his niche in working for the military as a civilian engineer.

Some years later, May moved into the digital field and accepted a secret project that brought him great pride and satisfaction. Admiral Rickover's Navy team had come to Indianapolis and asked May and his digital design team to develop equipment for making usable images and improving data processing from the transoceanic underwater cable that ran from St. Petersburg to Vladivostok, Russia.

May 2005.

Charles and Jane on their 60ᵗʰ anniversary in 2011.

May explained, "The U.S. Navy located the Russian's cable and found it was not encrypted. They developed a small submarine called the fish and the tethering mechanisms, but two low light level TV's were not useable because of the noise. Our job was to make the images useable and improve the data processing."

It proved to be a very successful undertaking for May and his team. "The equipment was used for the rest of the '70s, '80s and early '90s," May said with pride. "The United States knew all of the Russian military secrets, and the Russians weren't any the wiser." He added, "I am glad and proud to have been a small part of what contributed to global peace."

May met his wife, Vivian Jane Thompson, while he was at Purdue University. The two married on September 20, 1951 and moved to Martinsville in 1963. Their marriage was blessed with 3 children: Mark, Jo Ellen and Lou Anne. The extended family now includes 6 grandchildren and 3 great-great grandchildren. The couple celebrated their 60ᵗʰ Wedding Anniversary in 2011.

By the time May retired from Naval Avionics he had received 5 patents on radar technology. Since retirement he has written his own autobiography (*Life's Events*, a 257 page book) and has contributed articles on electronics as well as space & universe. He enjoys collecting rocks, traveling, gardening, and continues to enjoy the company of his wife and his family.

May, holding his autobiography.

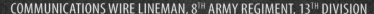

A Perfect Life in War and Peace

Veteran Reflects on Combat and Life

"It's been a perfect life," said Oscar McClure of Danville, Indiana, looking back at his 89 years. And, by his recollection, that description includes the 17 months he lived in a combat zone during World War II.

McClure was part of the 8th Army Division, 13th Regiment that was fighting its way across Europe in 1944 during some challenging conditions.

Born on June 1, 1925, he was drafted into the Army in June of 1943. "I had a few teary nights," he said, reflecting on his time at boot camp.

Following his basic training he was sent to Camp Gruber, Oklahoma where he received training to be a communications wire lineman. He also was trained as a canoneer on a 37 mm canon and as a machine gunner.

Training at Camp Gruber lasted from September of 1943 until May of 1944 and included an infiltration course with live ammunition, house-to-house combat training, and field courses in the foothills of the Ozark Mountains of Arkansas.

By May of 1944, McClure was on his way to combat via the *U.S.S Aquitania* troop transport. After stops in Scotland and England, he reached Omaha Beach on June 10, 1944 — four days after the D-day invasion. He was among the first replacements for members of the 8th Army Division that had been killed during the initial landing.

Oscar wearing his "found" helmet.

McClure recalled his first night on Omaha Beach, "We were told to dig in. I borrowed a shovel from a soldier in the engineer company to dig my foxhole."

The next morning they headed into the hedgerows of Northwestern France and into combat.

Early in his combat experience, McClure sustained an arm injury from anti-aircraft fire. He was taken to the aid station and bandaged up. It was a sufficient enough wound to earn him a Purple Heart.

He remembered well the attention he received from his Company Commander, Captain John O'Hearn, Jr.

"He looked after me like I was his son," McClure said with deep emotion.

While taking a break one day in France, McClure lost his "steel" (a term used for the helmet each soldier wore) when it was accidentally knocked into the well he was sitting on. He eventually found another one to wear, but it had a bullet hole in it — an ominous image for the imminent risk of combat. He wore it for the rest of war.

When he wasn't laying or repairing communication lines, McClure served as a battalion runner, taking messages from the front line to the rear echelon headquarters element. Traveling back and forth meant assuming the risk of becoming a target for the enemy.

Danger was never far away. While moving through France, McClure recalled an occasion when two mortar shells landed right near his position. They would have certainly caused injury or death. Fortunately, they were both duds and failed to explode.

On another occasion, he was sleeping in a barn loft somewhere in France. He suddenly woke up to a fire. He grabbed his gun and went down to the main floor. The barn collapsed shortly thereafter. Someone had brought in field kitchen equipment and it had caught the straw in the loft on fire.

His regiment pushed its way across France and into Belgium. While there he recalled staying in a house on the 2nd floor. In the middle of the night he awoke to a disturbance. He discovered that a bomb shell had landed in the house and was lying under a table near him. "I skirted the table and shot down the steps," he said. "It was a dud, thank goodness!"

From Belgium his regiment pushed into Luxembourg and finally into Germany. And that was where the combat became really intense as McClure and his regiment found themselves participating in the Battle of the Hurtgen Forest.

Located along the border of Belgium and Germany, the 50 square mile area was a hilly region with dense forest. From mid-September through mid-December of 1944 (just before the Battle of the Bulge), U.S. and German forces were involved in a series of fierce battles that became the longest battle on German ground during World War II.

"Enemy shells would hit the trees and shower you with pieces of wood." McClure recalled of the battles in the forest, "It was a rough place!"

It was a place made even rougher by the blanket of deep snow, which often reached depths of 2 to 3 feet!

There were heavy losses of men on both sides of the fight. Over 33,000 U.S. forces became casualties to injury or death. McClure's beloved company commander was

Soldiers moving through the Hurtgen Forest.

one of them. Capt. O'Hearn, Jr. lost his life during that battle. "There isn't a day that goes by that I don't think of him," McClure said sadly.

The U.S. forces eventually took Cologne and crossed the Rhine River, where they met up with the Russians and learned of Germany's surrender.

"It was great," McClure exclaimed, regarding the war's end! "You just can't imagine the feeling of it!

We had taken thousands of prisoners and we had to just wave them back. They were very beat up and sad people. The German soldiers and people were happy it was over. The people of Germany were friendly and waved U.S. flags."

After Germany's surrender, McClure accepted the Army's offer to be trained as a cook. With a likely transfer to the Pacific Theater of combat, McClure figured it would be better for him to serve in the relative safety of a field kitchen then on the front lines. He was later promoted to Tech Sergeant.

"It was a great experience," McClure said concerning his time in the service. "I wouldn't trade it for anything in the world. I'm proud I was able to do what I was asked. So much (good) for so little (time/sacrifice)!"

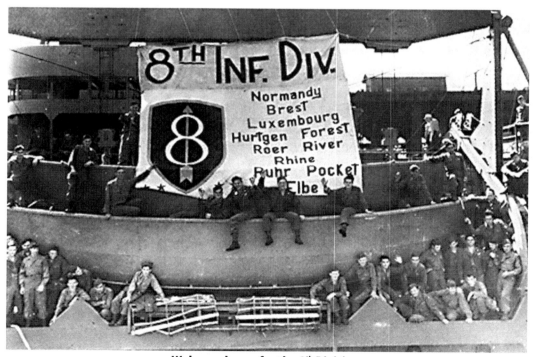

Welcome home for the 8th Division.

When his time of service was completed, McClure boarded the *U.S.S Grant* troop transport and headed home to the U.S. He served as cook at Fort Leonard Wood, Missouri, until he was discharged at Fort Knox, Kentucky in November of 1945. He came home and surprised his parents at the door.

McClure started the next chapter of his life back home working at a grocery store for 1.5 years for $32 per week. He was then offered a job at Capitol Paper Company as an appliance repairman for $78 per week. In 1950, he opened McClure Appliance Service. He operated the business until he retired in July of 2011 at the age of 86, after 65 years of labor.

By his estimates, he did appliance work in 50,000 or more homes during his working years.

His most memorable service call

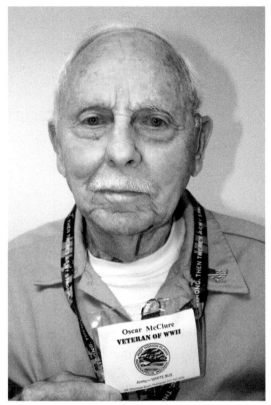

Oscar on an Honor Flight.

involved being held hostage inside a home by a man convicted of manslaughter. McClure kept his cool and was released after a time.

In addition to working, McClure also found time to build three different homes, digging the foundations with a shovel.

He met his first wife, Patricia Louise (Patty Lou), after the war in September of 1946. They married a short time later. "She was perfect," he said with deep fondness. Together they raised six children: four boys and two girls.

The family moved to Danville, Indiana in 1972, where McClure has lived ever since. At one point after moving into their new home he recalled his wife looking at him and saying, "Don't you just love the way we're living?" The couple enjoyed almost 50 years before Patty Lou's death in January 29, 1998. "We had a perfect life," he said.

McClure married his second wife, Nancy Hall, four years later. She died in January of 2010.

Oscar and one of his radio-controlled boats.

McClure has spent much of his free time since retirement, and the deaths of his wives, building radio controlled boats and planes. "It's what kept me alive," he said. Two of the boats are named for his deceased wives.

Loving to do for others, he also makes jelly and cookies and then gives them away as gifts to family, friends and former customers.

"I've had the best life of anyone in the world," he said.

McClure's 'perfect life' came to a close on January 15, 2015, at the age of 89.

Oscar and one the planes he built.

Back and Forth Duty

Veteran Traverses the Atlantic on a Troop Transport

Most World War II veterans who fought in the European theater crossed the Atlantic Ocean twice; once to get to their combat location and once to get home. Charlie Miller made the trip 8 times, courtesy of the U.S. Navy!

Miller, a native of Indianapolis, enlisted in the Navy in late 1944 after graduating from Broad Ripple High School. Following his training as a Seaman, he was assigned to the *USS Lejeune*, a former German luxury liner that had been acquired by the U.S. during its internment in Brazil and later converted into a troop transport ship.

It was a most unlikely transformation for the ship (formerly the *USS Windhoek*). Not only had it belonged to Germany, but the German crew, prior to abandoning

USS LeJeune.

the vessel, had also done everything possible to make it unusable. "The Germans poured concrete into the engines," Miller explained. The crippled vessel lay dormant in Brazil for two years before repairs were made and the U.S. gained control of it.

The ship had two swimming pools, weighed 19,200 tons and was 510 feet long.

Following her repair and refit the newly named *USS Lejeune* had the capacity to carry 4,000 troops and had spaces for 500 crewmembers and officers. In a twist of irony, during one of her earliest trips from Europe, the ship brought German POW's to the United States.

Miller's first crossing of the Atlantic on the transport was in June of 1945. The *Lejeune* was part of a large convoy of ships making the crossing. Although the war in Europe had officially ended, there was still the threat of German U-boat activity in the Atlantic. "It scared the sh*t out of me!" exclaimed Miller. "There weren't that many U-boats still around, but the threat of them was enough of a scare!"

The convoy traveled fast at 20 knots and arrived safely in LeHarve, France where they picked up a load of troops. "Most of the time we brought them home through the port in New York City," Miller said.

Early in his service Miller's job was chipping paint. But after a few months he got into the supply department and served as the "Jack of Dust" — keeping track of canned food inventories on ship. The position included enjoying an office all to himself.

One highlight during his service was a trip to Paris, France. While his ship was undergoing two weeks of repair at a French port, Miller arranged for a "port/

USS *LeJeune* (AP-74), ship dance, Hotel Towers, New York. January 3, 1945.

starboard" five-day tour in Paris, paid for out of the ships fund.

The most memorable of Miller's eight crossings was in December of 1945. The ship was in Bremerhaven, Germany picking up another load of troops for their return home. While waiting for the departure date, Miller had a chance to walk to town. "It was the most beat up place I had ever

Boarding *USS LeJeune*, leaving France 1945.

seen," he recalled of the area inland from the port. "You had to walk three miles before seeing a section of wall that remained intact on a building."

The ship departed Bremerhaven on Christmas Eve of 1945. As the ship got underway Miller remembered a spontaneous eruption of Christmas carols being sung. "You could almost feel the vibration of the singing throughout the ship," he remembered. "It was just really wonderful!"

Miller received his discharge shortly after returning to the States in January of 1946. He enrolled at Butler University, but he remained in the Navy Reserve.

Having known since age 14 that he wanted to be in journalism, Miller pursued a career in the field and worked for several different newspapers, including the *Indianapolis Times*.

By 1951, he was back on active duty, recalled for service during the Korean Conflict. Having already established himself as a civilian journalist, he was assigned to the Navy's media outreach team. Working from Evanston, IL he wrote military news releases for small town newspapers. "It was the Navy's first real outreach to the small, hometown media," recalled Miller.

Journalism remained Miller's passion and profession for the next several decades. He worked at the city desk for the *Indianapolis Times*, served as a reporter in Palmetto, FL and wrote features for the *Martinsville Reporter-Times*. He also had stints in corporate public relations. Highlights from his profession include writing stories on Billy Graham crusades in the 1950s, interviewing several U.S. Presidents and writing a first edition of published articles on "Medicare and You," which is still read and used today. Miller officially retired in 1993.

In 1991, Miller organized the first reunion for those who served on the *USS LeJeune*.

Miller, Honor Flight Homecoming in 2012.

Looking back over his time of service Miller said, "It was a real adventure at 17-18 years of age! But as you get older you wonder about the other guys who paid so much and you wonder, 'Why was I so lucky?'"

Miller recalled seeing the burial site of the 'unlucky' ones. Gazing over the large fields of white crosses dotting the landscape in northern France he said, "There would be two kinds of crosses. They would be separated; the Germans over here, and the Americans and British over there." Following some silent reflection he added, "That's always given me pause."

Such thoughts often bring Miller back to a memory of his cousin. "My cousin was in World War I," he said. "And he, every year — he was in the Battle of the Somme and was seriously injured — every year on Armistice Day he'd sit and read this," he said, while pulling out a printed copy of the poem, "In Flanders Fields" by John McCrae. "That made a big impression on me," he concluded.

In Flanders fields the poppies blow;
Between the crosses, row on row,
That mark our place; and in the sky
The larks, still bravely singing, fly
Scarce heard amid the guns below...

Miller lives in Martinsville with his wife and continues to do some writing in retirement.

Let Her Fly!
Veteran Launches Planes and Golf Balls

James D. Rees has watched thousands of golf balls take flight from the striking face of his golf club. But it isn't the only thing he has hurled into the sky. During World War II, he had a hand in launching something far more important — hundreds of planes from the catapult on his ship.

Born James Dwire Rees, Jr. in Maysville, Kentucky on March 28, 1920, he was the youngest of three children raised by his parents, James and Mary (Pyles) Rees. The family lived in Canada and Florida before settling in Indiana.

After graduating from Tech High School in Indianapolis in 1938 he attended the University of Kentucky for two years. In 1940 he returned to Indianapolis and worked as a greens keeper at Willow Brook Golf Club on Keystone Avenue. His father was leasing the land and had begun managing the course.

Suspecting he was going to be drafted, he enlisted in the Navy on December 1, 1941 — just six days prior to the Japanese attack on Pearl Harbor. "Right then my life turned around," he said, remembering his sudden transition into leadership and responsibility for others.

Rees recalled, "Since I was 21 years old and had two years of college, I was older than the rest of the mostly 17-18 year old young men. I was put in charge of 60 of them and was told to take them to The Great Lakes Training Station." It was an early indication of the leadership that Rees would be entrusted with in the days ahead.

Rees in Willow Brook truck.

Rees wanted to be a pilot, but he was informed that he was two college credit hours short of qualifying for pilot training. So he entered the Navy as an apprentice seaman, grateful that he would be spared from the Army's typical trench warfare.

Following his basic training at Great Lakes Naval Training Center, Rees spent six months completing his Aviation Machinist's Mate schooling. Then he and several others were sent to the Philadelphia Navy Yard for his 4 weeks of catapult training.

By the summer of 1942, he was on a cross-country trip by train to Bremerton, Washington, where he met up with the *USS Bogue* (CVE-9), a brand new escort aircraft carrier that was still getting her final touches before being commissioned. Rees started training with the catapult on the flight deck.

One day, while sitting on the steps leading down to the catapult compartment, Rees was approached by a Navy Chief who asked him if he wanted to run the catapult. Not wanting to turn down the Chief, he accepted the appointment.

"It was my biggest move," he said looking back at the opportunity. It was also probably his most dangerous move, though he didn't know it at the time!

The catapult compartment housed the machinery that controlled the build-up and release of 3,000 pounds of hydraulic oil pressure that moved the cylinder on

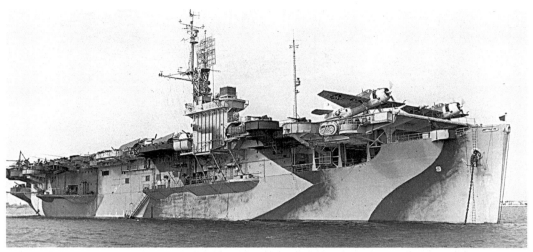

USS *Bogue* at Bermuda, 1945.

deck to 'catapult' the planes into the skies. If anything went wrong down in the compartment, the highly pressurized oil could easily explode, likely killing anyone in the room.

The catapult crew consisted of five men. They all wore different color of shirts. Rees wore green. Four of the crew members were on deck with the plane, while Rees was inside the compartment. It was his job to read the pressure gauges and control the lever, which released the valve and caused the build-up and release of the pressurized hydraulic oil. "They gave me flight pay," he recalled, "because if something went wrong; I was dead."

The catapult track was 75 feet long and had a cylinder shuttle that ran down the deck as it pulled the plane forward. Every time a plane was launched the cable became loose and the crew had to retrieve and reset it.

When the *USS Bogue* was finally ready for combat service, she left Bremerton and arrived in San Diego where she received her complement of planes. The ship then traveled east and passed through the Panama Canal. Rees recalled, "I sat on the flight deck all the way watching the ship go up and down through the canals and locks." (While sitting on the deck, he also got the worst sunburn of his life.) From her entrance into the Caribbean Sea the ship moved east to the Atlantic Ocean and up the eastern coast to Norfolk, Virginia, where it was fitted with anti-aircraft guns.

The *USS Bogue* was the main ship in the anti-submarine patrol group. She traversed the Atlantic Ocean leading convoys of Allied ships across the Atlantic to

Aircraft launch from catapult.

Ireland or Scotland, all the while looking for enemy submarines. When she found them, she released her planes to bomb them from above.

Rees remembered, "When we first went over we could only fly during the daytime. We could cover the ocean one mile wide and seventy miles out just before dark. Then they developed landing lights down the sides of the landing deck, allowing us to fly at night. The light was green when planes were coming in safely, yellow when the planes were too high and red when the planes were too low."

Before long, the *USS Bogue* was flying anti-submarine patrols 24-hours a day. "The planes carried six hours of gas," Rees said. "So, the flights were every four hours. We would sleep between flights. We arranged one day off every 28 days."

Rees and the other four men of the crew were berthed in the catapult compartment. "Every four hours a plane was going up," he recalled of the hectic schedule. "One night, I had to get up five times because German subs were following our convoy."

When enemy subs were spotted, the *USS Bogue* sent up a plane which would locate the sub, fly right over it and drop a depth charge, a torpedo or a sonar buoy. "We could hear the explosion and see oil and debris on the surface," Rees recalled. "We never got any survivors from the enemy subs." (Aircraft Carriers didn't pick up the survivors, if there were any. Other ships in the convoy did that. Ships couldn't officially count the sinking of a sub unless they brought back survivors to prove it. And lots of times there weren't any survivors.)

The most exciting day for Rees and the crew on the *U.S.S. Bogue* was May 15, 1944, when 10 German U-boats were closing in on the *USS Bogue*. The planes from the USS Bogue and the Destroyer guard in the convoy sunk nine of the U-boats. Rees witnessed one of the German submarines getting

Deck crews of the Bogue try to recover a crashed Avenger from the catwalk. June 19, 1944.

blasted away. The submarine had just started to surface when one of the planes that Rees had earlier launched into the sky located the sub and dropped a depth charge

on it. "The water from the charge came up 100 feet. And when the water came back down there was no submarine left. That was that. It was the most exciting day of my life!" exclaimed Rees.

The ship and crew enjoyed great success in their mission. During her two and a half years of combat service, she supported the sinking of 13 enemy submarines — 11 German subs and two of Japanese origin. She made 14 trips across the Atlantic and never lost a ship in her convoy. For her stellar performance the *Bogue* received the Presidential Unit Citation and three battle stars.

Rees receiving Presidential Citation.

Jim and Peggy's wedding day.

Following his discharge in September of 1945, Rees returned home to his wife, Peggy, whom he had married while on furlough just before leaving for combat.

He recalled, "I went home and the next day my father called and asked me what I was doing and I said I thought I would take a month off. He said, 'No! Get out here (Willow Brook Golf Club) and get the greens mowed. I did, but since I had not worked that hard for four years, the next day I could hardly get out of bed."

James and Peggy went on to raise four children: Esther, Dan, Sara and Ginger. His family has grown to include seven grandchildren and 8 great-grandchildren.

Rees loved the golf course business and began searching in Marion County for land to buy to convert to a golf course.

Rees' father died in February of 1946, not long after he was discharged from the Navy. His mother, and his sisters ran Willow Brook until

Dan, Esther, Peggy, Jim in back, Ginger and Sara in front.

Jim and Peggy at Friendswood.

the landlord sold the property to a developer and the golf course had to close in 1966. His sisters and their families went north to operate Sycamore Springs Golf Course. Rees had bought the Camby property in 1962 and started Friendswood Golf Course. Rees moved his family there in 1966 when Willow Brook closed. He and his wife managed the course for twenty years until his retirement in 1986. Sara manages the course today with her son, David.

In 1990 he married his second wife, Alice Rose York.

Rees has remained active in retirement. For many years he restored Model T Fords. He was a ham radio operator and even taught students at the Indiana School for the Blind how to operate the radios. He is a charter member of the Eagle Creek Sailing Club and helped build many of the docks. And he was active at the Mooresville Senior Center, serving as a board member for several years.

Today Rees enjoys life from the comfort of his apartment in Plainfield, Indiana. He doesn't launch things much anymore, but he still has a putter and is known to practice tapping the ball into the metallic cup on his living room floor. Even after all these years, he still likes to send things in motion.

Jim points to his ship on a USS Bogue *plaque.*

S.S. Jeremiah O'Brien, liberty ship.

Supply Runs to Europe
The Dangerous Crossings of U.S. Cargo Ships

Crossing the Atlantic Ocean was not an unusual experience for those who fought in the European Theater during World War II. Most soldiers and sailors arrived in Europe on a ship. And most of them returned back to the U.S. on a ship. But some men made the dangerous transit across the Atlantic much more often. Fredrick Robinson Jr. of Martinsville, Indiana was one of them.

The life-long Morgan county resident was born on Christmas Eve of 1924. He was raised in Centerton, Indiana and attended school in nearby Martinsville. After completing high school in 1943, he enlisted in the Navy and was sworn in on the Post Office steps in downtown Indianapolis.

"THERE SHALL BE NO SURRENDER SO LONG AS THE GUNS CAN BE FOUGHT"
The United States Naval Armed Guards of WWII

Although he could have stayed home and helped on the farm with his dad, he felt like he had a responsibility to serve. "Besides," he said, "my enlistment saved one guy from the draft board."

Following three weeks of boot camp at Great Lakes Naval Training Center he attended one week of gunnery school in Norfolk, Virginia and became qualified as gun "trainer". Ship gun crews had 2 men operating each gun. The trainer moved the gun up and down and was responsible for finding the area. The "pointer" moved the guns sideways and zeroed in on the exact target. Both men had to pull the trigger for the gun to fire.

Following his training, Robinson was assigned as a member of the Navy Armed Guards, a unit that supplied gun crews on special cargo ships of the US Merchant Marine. These ships, often referred to as "Liberty" or "Victory" ships, were built in the U.S. during World War II and were designed to replace the regular cargo ships in Europe that were constantly being sunk by German U-boats. This newer class of cargo ships was outfitted with Navy guns to help defend against German attack by water or air while crossing the Atlantic with important supplies for the war effort.

The typical Liberty ship had a crew of 25 consisting of 1 officer and 24 crew, mostly gunners (although the crew could be as many as 45 if combat was likely) and was outfitted with one 5-inch/38 caliber gun in the stern, one 3-inch/50 caliber gun in the bow and usually eight 20 mm guns secured at several places around the ship. From 1941 to 1945, the United States built and employed a staggering 3,241 "Liberty" and "Victory" cargo ships.

Robinson's first assignment was on the *SS Elihu Yale,* which departed from the Brooklyn Naval Yards for Europe on December 24, 1943 — the same day as Fredrick's 19th birthday. The last of his teen years would be spent in the dangerous waters of the European theater of war.

As cargo ships of the Merchant Marine could travel no faster than 10 knots, transit across the Atlantic Ocean usually took about ten days. Once the ship arrived in England or France it would take two weeks or so to offload the supplies of food, gasoline and/or small arm ammunition, which would be trucked inland to sustain the Allied troops. When the French coast was finally opened following D-Day, the cargo ships were able to go directly to France for unloading.

Once unloaded, the ship would either return to the United States for another load of supplies bound for Europe or shuttle supply loads across the English Channel between Scotland and France. Robinson recalled spending six months crisscrossing the English Channel between France and Scotland following the opening of France after D-Day. Glasgow, Scotland and Belfast, Ireland had important supply bases from which food, fuel and ammunition were picked up and delivered to the war fronts.

Throughout that first year of transits and deliveries Robinson and the crew on board the *SS Elihu Yale* managed to stay safe. But all of that changed in early 1944 as they passed through the Mediterranean Sea near Italy.

On February 15, 1944, the cargo ship was approximately 2 miles off the coast of the Anzio, Italy's beachhead — the same beach that the U.S. Fifth Army had secured during the Allied Landing a few weeks earlier on January 22, 1944. The secured beachhead did not, however, guarantee a secured sea lane, as the crew of the *Elihu Yale* found out. German fighter planes from the *Luftwaffe* were flying overhead

Armed guard crew on guns.

patrolling the coast when one of them noticed the *Elihu Yale*. The plane descended and dropped one of its aerial bombs — directing it at the ship. The glide bomb hit the stern of the ship and threw Fredrick, on the fantail at the time, and many other crew members into the water. The damage to the ship was significant, and she quickly sank into the sea.

Of the 45 Navy Armed Guard crewmen on board the ship, only 18 of them survived the sinking. Robinson was one of the fortunate ones. There were also 40 merchant marine crewmen on the ship. It is not known how many of them survived.

Robinson and others were picked up while floating in the sea by a British sub chaser. The survivors were then dropped off on the beach near Anzio, with no clothing. They had shed most of their clothes to avoid being weighed down by wet clothes. Members of the Fifth Army Division that remained at the beachhead took care of them — giving them food, shelter and clothing. They remained near the beach and waited for the next 4-5 weeks before finally getting on board the *USS General A.E. Anderson,* an Army Transport Troopship, to catch a ride back to the United States. During the trip back they were assigned to care for patients who were also being transported stateside.

After his return to the U.S., Robinson attended Advanced Gunnery School — a four-week course in Norfolk, Virginia. Following his advanced training, he was assigned to another cargo ship with the Merchant Marine and resumed the famil-

SS George Washington Carver.

SS George Eldridge.

iar transit of the resupply route across the Atlantic between the U.S. and Europe. He served out the remainder of the war on the *SS George Eldridge* and the *SS George Washington Carver*.

Fredrick wasn't the only Robinson boy to serve in the Armed Forces during World War II. Like many families at that time there were multiple sons and even daughters who joined the armed forces. In the Robinson family Fredrick joined the Navy, Bob and Bill served in the Army, and brother Jay was in the Army Air Force. The other Robinson brother was unable to serve because he'd had infantile paralysis.

On February 25, 1946 Fredrick was discharged from active duty. Wanting to continue his service he joined the Navy Reserve and drilled out of the Indianapolis Reserve Center. He served for another nine years, from 1946–1955, before finally hanging up his uniform for good. In 1958, he tried to re-enlist, but the Navy wouldn't take him. Looking back on his service in the U.S. Navy Robinson said, "I'd do it again."

Robinson married his wife, Sarah, in January of 1951. Their marriage of over 60 years was blessed with a daughter, Cathy. Robinson retired from Chevrolet in 1980 having worked as a mechanic and later as a general supervisor.

Robinson died at the age of 89 on January 16, 2014. He was buried at the Centerton Cemetery in Morgan County, Indiana. He was a 50-year member of both the American Legion and the Veterans of Foreign Wars.

Frederick Robinson, Jr.

A Love for Flying

Paratrooper Ascends to the Skies in Service and in Life

Most people are content to live out their lives on the ground. Max Shanklin has preferred to spend a good portion of his life in the air.

Shanklin was born on March 23, 1923 in Indianapolis, Indiana. He was one of four children raised by his parents, Charles and Ethel Shanklin.

After graduating from Decatur Central High School in 1941, Shanklin found work as a bottle washer at Eli Lilly Company.

Suspecting that he would be drafted soon, he decided to enlist in 1942. Having an interest in aviation from childhood, he enrolled in the Navy Aviation Cadet Program. After his basic training in Chicago he returned to Indianapolis for three months of civilian pilot training at Weir Cook Airport. From there he went to Monterrey, California for three months of pre-flight training and then Hutchinson, Kansas for primary flight training.

During flight training, Shanklin honed another one of his skills — boxing. He became pretty good at it and enjoyed some success in the amateur rings.

While in Hutchinson, one of the guys in his squad mentioned to Shanklin that his brother was in the Merchant Marine program and was making a lot of money.

The Navy was paying $75 a month. The Merchant Marines were offering men $400-$500 month. Shanklin decided to temporarily put his dreams for the air on hold and chase the money to be made on the water.

He and seven others left the Navy and entered Merchant Marine Training in Sheepshead Bay, Brooklyn, NY.

After completing his basic training he was invited to go to junior officer school in St. Petersburg, Florida. Following his three months of training there he was sent to New Orleans to be assigned to one of the merchant ships that would be heading out to the South Pacific.

He waited for three months in New Orleans, but he was never assigned to a ship. There were more junior officers than there were positions available for them.

Having seen a poster on a bulletin board promoting direct commission opportunities in the Army, Shanklin decided once again to leave one service and enter another. His service journey — from Naval Aviation to Merchant Marine to the Army — seemed to be taking him further away from the skies. Or so he thought.

Shanklin at jump school.

He accepted a direct commission into the Army as a 2nd Lieutenant and began his eight weeks of basic officer training in Tallahassee, Florida. While there, he saw another poster. This one promoted the need for paratroopers with the words, *"Jump into the Fight!"* Shanklin had found his ticket back into the skies!

He went to Ft. Benning, Georgia for Basic Infantry Training and then entered Jump School — the five-week training that prepared him to leap out of planes and descend through the skies via parachute.

Following his training, Shanklin was assigned to the 515th Parachute Infantry Regiment, which became part of the 13th Airborne Division. In January of 1945 he boarded a ship and headed to France.

The Regimental Headquarters were located in Auxerre, France — a city southeast of Paris. From there, Shanklin's unit continued their airborne training and awaited their combat mission. But it never came. By that point in the war, the Allied Forces were moving toward Germany with little resistance and paratroopers were not needed.

During some down time, Shanklin explored Paris. He ascended the Eifel Tower and toured the cathedral of Notre Dame. "For a kid raised poor, who had never been anywhere, I saw a lot in Europe," he recalled.

His was one of the first units to leave Europe after Germany's surrender. The plan was to return to the U.S. for a 30-day leave and then head over to the Pacific theater. But while Shanklin was enjoying his visit home the war in the Pacific ended.

Shanklin separated from military service and returned home to his wife, Violet, whom he had married in 1942. His son, Max was born in 1945.

Shanklin jumping from plane.

He began working again at Eli Lilly and enrolled at Butler University, graduating with a degree in Business and Advertising.

In October of 1950, the Army recalled him from the inactive reserve for 17 months of service in Korea. "There was no re-familiarization training," he lamented. "Twenty-nine of the thirty-one of us were sent to Korea, and many of them were killed."

Shanklin, now a Lieutenant, arrived in Japan and was initially assigned as an Assistant Detachment Officer at a hospital in Fukuoka on the island of Kyushu, Japan.

A year later, he was transferred to the 187th Regimental Combat Team in Korea, where he became a mortar platoon leader and spent six months in combat. "I had never been around a mortar in my whole life," Shanklin exclaimed! The man who aspired to fly the skies suddenly found himself launching mortars into them.

Mortar team in Korea.

His unit was constantly being sent out to help other units that were pinned down in combat. "I got scared a few times over there," he added.

He also got a Purple Heart for wounds that he sustained in combat.

His unit rotated back to Japan, where Shanklin became the Assistant Public Information Officer and finished his recall time.

Since he had a degree, Shanklin could have elected to go into the regular Army and make a career of it. He would have done so, but his wife didn't want him to. So, he returned home and, in 1953, his daughter, Karen, was born.

During that same year, Shanklin got his private pilot's license and began flying on his own. After a while, he purchased his own plane. He would own several of them in the years ahead. He started making some extended solo flights — his longest being a trip out to Oregon.

Shanklin points to a photo of himself flying a plane.

Shanklin beside plane he is building.

Shanklin once again went back to Eli Lilly Company. He climbed the corporate ladder and became a supervisor and finally a department head. From 1968 to 1971 he moved to Fresno, California, where he helped set up a distribution center for Lilly.

In 1971 he also married his second wife, Sherry.

His love for aviation continued to grow, expanding from flying planes to actually building them. Over the years he has built 12 planes from kits and repaired 5 other planes that were wrecked. Today, at the age of 91, he's still building *and* flying them.

His most recent flight, however, was not as a pilot but as a passenger. He was one of the 70 veterans that left from Indianapolis in May of 2014 on the Indy Honor Flight trip to Washington D.C. "It was great!" he exclaimed. "A once-in-a-lifetime opportunity!"

And speaking of lifetimes, there is a plaque next to a framed collage of photos of Shanklin and his many planes. The plaque reads: *Time spent flying is not deducted from one's lifetime.* If that is the case, Shanklin may very well have a long life yet to live!

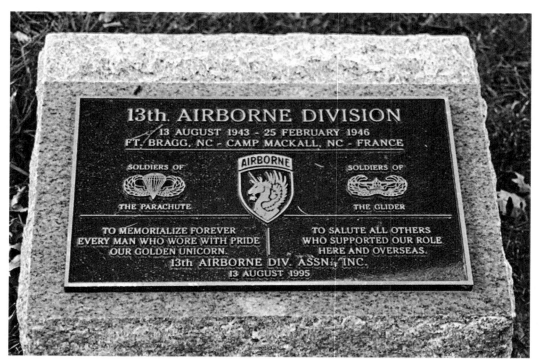

13th Airborne Division memorial, Arlington National Cemetery.

Riding the High Seas

Sailor on USS Nevada *saw action in Atlantic and Pacific Theaters*

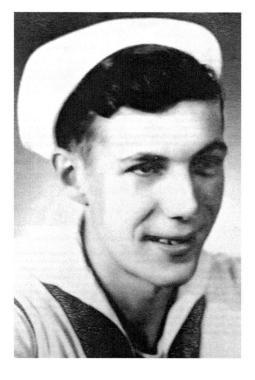

Not many Navy ships served in both the Atlantic and Pacific theaters of World War II. The Battleship *USS Nevada*, the only Battleship to get underway during the attack on the Pacific fleet at Pearl Harbor, was one of them. And Paul Shaerer, of Plainfield, Indiana, was one of her proud 2,000-member crew.

Born in Clayton, New Jersey, Shaerer entered the service in June of 1943, as a selective volunteer following his graduation from high school. "I knew as a youth that something had to be done," he recalled of his decision to enlist.

When asked why he chose the Navy he replied, "Three meals a day and a bed to sleep in!"

Following his boot camp in Bainbridge, Maryland, Shaerer traveled to Boston and reported for duty as a seaman on the *USS Nevada*, where he was assigned as a loader for the 20 mm guns. It would be his home for the next three years.

The *USS Nevada*, nicknamed the "Cheer Up Ship," had been launched in July of 1914 and had served in the last couple of months of World War I. She was the first battleship of the U.S. Navy to sport triple gun turrets. Although she was able to escape Pearl Harbor and get underway during the Japanese attack, she did suffer significant damage from 6 bomb hits and one torpedo hit. She was grounded just off Ford Island until repairs could be made back at Pearl Harbor.

Nevada supporting the landings on Utah Beach, 6 June 1944.

When Shaerer arrived on the ship in 1943, the *USS Nevada* was on Atlantic Convoy duty, accompanying and protecting supply ships going back and forth from New York to England. "We were in the center and there were 50-60 ships all around us," said Shaerer. "We made that trip four times. And then we stayed in the English Channel at Normandy." It was April of 1944 and the Allied ships were getting in position to support the D-day landing.

The *Nevada* went up and down the Normandy coastline shooting its 14-inch shells inland to support the landing forces. The shells traveled 14 miles inland, accurately hitting the German shore defenses.

After its work in Normandy, the *USS Nevada* headed for the Mediterranean Sea to support Allied landings at Toulon in Southern France. She served from August 15 to September 25, 1944 and was instrumental in helping bring down the heavily armed coastal fortress used by the Germans.

After having some of her guns replaced in New York, the *Nevada* traveled westward toward the Pacific theater, passing through the Panama Canal. "The difference between the Atlantic and the Pacific," remarked Shaerer, "is that the Atlantic is choppy and the Pacific rolls up and down."

The *Nevada* reached her destination of Iwo Jima on February 16, 1945 and prepared for the pre-landing bombardment. Shaerer recalled, "We got in so close (to the island) once or twice during our bombardment that we got word that the 14-inch shells were hitting the beach sand, projecting over

Nevada bombarding Iwo Jima, 19 February 1945.

the island and going into the water on the other side. So, we backed up and raised our guns a little bit."

By March 24, 1945, the *Nevada* had joined Task Force 54 and moved into place to provide fire-support for the Marines' landing on the island of Okinawa. On March 25th, the crew awakened to discover a brand new horror — the emergence of the Japanese Kamikazes! Seven of them attacked the Task Force and one of them successfully crashed into the *Nevada's* deck.

40 mm guns firing at kamikazes.

Shaerer remembered, "It was coming directly toward the bridge. Some of our guns knocked off its left wing, which turned it away from the bridge and down the side of the ship to the back where a group of Marines were firing 20 mm guns."

In the ensuing crash, 11 men were killed and 49 were wounded. "When we got back out at sea," Shaerer recalled, "the Chaplain had the body bags of the sailors and we dropped them into the sea." Among the bodies that were buried at sea was the Kamikaze pilot who had crashed his plane into the ship.

"They did damage," Shaerer said concerning the Kamikazes, "but (in the end) it didn't work!" And after a short pause, he concluded, "War is hell. But it has to be done."

The *Nevada* survived the Pacific War and returned to the United States in 1946. Shaerer was discharged as a 1st class Petty Officer and returned to New Jersey where he enrolled in college at Glassboro State Teacher's College (now Rowan University) and became a middle school teacher. After a few years of teaching he went back to school to get his principal's license and served as a New Jersey school principal for 30 years, before retiring in the mid-'80s.

Shaerer met his wife, Jean Watson, to whom he has been married for 63 years, in church after he returned from the war. They got married in 1949 and were blessed with two children: Gregg and Donna Jean. Since then, three grandchildren and five great-grandchildren have been added to their family.

Shaerer holds a photo of the USS Nevada's *crew.*

The couple spent 20 years of retirement living in Ocala, Florida before moving to Plainfield, Indiana to be closer to their daughter.

Reflecting back on his war years Shaerer concluded: "Being in the Navy was the best thing that ever happened to me. I grew up quickly. It was rough. I was away from home for three Thanksgivings and Christmases. But it was worth it. I was helping to save a lot of lives."

Shaerer was on the inaugural trip of Indy Honor Flight's trip to Washington DC in September of 2012.

Paul in front of WWII Memorial.

Paul (standing, second row, second from right in red shirt) at Crew Reunion.

USS Nevada Post-Script: Following her return from duty in World War 2, the near 33-year-old *USS Nevada* was slated for a final mission — that of serving as a target ship for the atomic experiments in 'Operation Crossroads'. The experiment was designed to test the effectiveness of atomic detonations on Naval ships. On July 26, 1946 two atomic

bombs were detonated with the *USS Nevada* in the bulls-eye. Probably to the surprise of none of her former crew, she proved to be difficult to sink! After surviving both atomic hits, she was taken in for further examination and then officially decommissioned on August 29, 1946. She was used one last time for gunnery practice in July of 1948 as the *Iowa* and two other Naval ships fired upon her. Once again, she refused to sink. It wasn't until an aerial torpedo was dropped upon her that she finally succumbed to her watery resting place.

USS Nevada during WWII.

**Her decks littered with dead, wounded, and debris,
an LCI comes along side *Nevada* for medical aid and
assistance. Battle for Iwo Jima, 17 February 1945.**

Heartache on the English Channel
Infantryman still mourns loss

December 24, 1944 was unlike any Christmas Eve that Loren Wright had ever experienced. On that night his regiment was crossing the English Channel in two ships. Wright's ship made it across safely. The other ship did not.

A deep heartache from the channel has been with him ever since.

Wright was born on March 6, 1926. He was the second oldest of four children raised by his parents, Paul and Beulah Wright, in rural Owen County, Indiana. He attended Patricksburg High School, graduating in 1944.

He was drafted into the Army on May 10th of that same year and reported to boot camp at Camp Blanding, Florida. "I was there in the hottest part of the summer. I thought it was going to kill me," Wright remarked! "I swore I would never go back (to Florida). Guess where my wife and I go every winter?" Wright said with a laugh. The couple has been going to Florida each winter since Wright retired in 1983.

Following his advanced infantry training in Fort Rucker, Alabama Wright received his orders to the Army's 66th Infantry Division, the 262nd Regiment. The men were slotted for combat duty in what would come to be known as "The Battle of the Bulge."

By November, Wright boarded a troop transport from New Jersey and crossed the Atlantic Ocean for South Hampton, England.

SS Chesire.

SS Leopoldville.

On the evening of December 24, 1944, his regiment was divided in half and boarded two troop transports, the *SS Cheshire* and the *SS Leopoldville*, which would carry them across the English Channel and deliver them to Cherbourg, France. The 66th Division was slotted to augment troops already engaged in the Battle of the Bulge.

During the crossing, *SS Leopoldville* was sunk by a German U-boat.

"I happened to be on the other ship," Wright said with a mixture of gratitude and sadness.

There were 2,235 American troops on board the *SS Leopoldville*, among them one half of Wright's 262nd Regiment. Eight hundred and two American soldiers of the 66th Division perished — either by going down with the ship or dying of injury or hypothermia while awaiting rescue in the frigid waters.

Wright recalled, "They couldn't get anyone out there to assist with rescue because of all the Christmas Eve parties that were going on." After a short pause he added, "Christmas Eve and Christmas Day have been somber for me ever since."

The men on the *SS Cheshire* knew that something happened when their ship's engines were cut and they drifted in total darkness, awaiting the dawn. "We all stayed on the deck with rifles, helmets and overcoats on," recalled Wright. "It was pretty cold!"

When the men finally learned that their sister transport ship had been sunk they were given strict orders not to write home about the tragedy or ever to speak to others about it. The Allied Commanders feared that the reaction of the American public to the sinking would have an adverse effect on the war effort. Details of the sinking remained classified by the War Department until 1958.[1]

---

[1] Even after the information on the sinking of the Leopold was declassified, no attempts were made by the Department of Defense to notify the families of the dead as to their whereabouts and how they died. Further information did not become available to the families until the discovery of the sunken ship in 1984 and the subsequent novels that were written about the disaster thereafter.

Wright didn't have much time to dwell on the disaster. The remaining members of the 66th Infantry Division, no longer of sufficient numbers to augment the forces in Belgium, were sent instead to the 'Lorient Pocket' on the western coast of France to relieve the 97th Division, which was engaged in combat with 50,000 German forces dug in there.

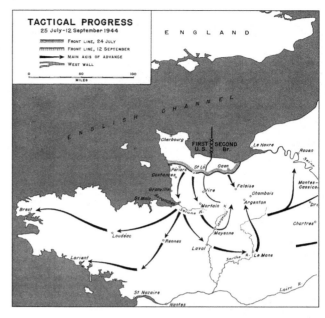

TACTICAL PROGRESS
25 July–12 September 1944

Wright spent the next 4 months on the Allied line in a foxhole designed for 3 people. The area was sandbagged and was right up against the added concealment of a hedgerow.

"We had telephone wire from the dugout to our artillery," said Wright. "We could communicate with them." That turned out to be especially helpful when Wright or his comrades thought they saw some movement in the darkness. They called on the artillery to shoot up a flare so that they could see what was out there ahead of them and fire if necessary.

"We received and returned fire a lot from the foxholes," recalled Wright. "During the day and the night"! He added, "We never slept at night. We had to protect our flanks. The Germans were trying to break out in places."

The standoff dragged on for four months. "They kept shooting at us and we kept shooting at them," he said. "We never knew when it was safe to get out of that hole. It was very hard on our nerves."

The Allied line of defense was close enough to the Germans that they could sometimes hear them. "We could hear their chuck wagons dropping off food for them," Wright added.

At times Wright and his comrades were sent into the German lines to make contact with them. "I got close to being hit on one of those occasions," exclaimed Wright! "It grazed my helmet."

Some of Wright's buddies were wounded and captured by the Germans. And some were killed.

Loren (left) and brother, Art, in Paris.

Loren in Paris.

Even when Wright wasn't in direct contact with the Germans, he was never far from their firepower. "They fired the 88's (big anti-aircraft artillery guns), which you couldn't hear until they detonated. It was demoralizing! You would just fall down wherever you could. Luckily, I didn't get hit!"

Wright remembers well the last day of combat on May 6th. "They opened up with everything they had day and night," he said. By the next day, it was all over. Germany had surrendered.

The men of the 66th were taken off the front lines and put on trucks for transport. They drove right past the German line and saw the Germans who had surrendered and large piles of German weapons that had been relinquished by the enemy.

When things quieted down Wright did get the chance to go to Paris on a R&R trip and meet his older brother, Art, who was serving there as a baker. "We had a ball," he said!

After a brief stint of occupation duty in Germany, the 66th Division was sent to Marseilles, France to help process troops that were leaving for home or preparing to be shipped to the Pacific theater. Wright worked in the field kitchen tents. His duties were to keep the fires going which were used to heat water for cleaning. He also delivered food and observed the men passing through the lines at meals to ensure portion control.

While he was there, he was able to enjoy a visit from Bob Hope and his orchestra that was on tour.

Wright finished his time of service with the 42nd Division in Austria, guarding supply depots at a railroad yard in Vienna. He then found a typing job in Linz.

During his service in Austria he had the opportunity to see the countryside. "Vienna is a beautiful place," he said! "Mountains all around it!"

But not all of his travels were for fun. He also took a trip to Southern France to visit the grave of a cousin who had died in the Battle of the Bulge.

Before he left Austria, he also received a unique gift. A German POW made a rainbow ring for Wright out of a toothbrush. He still has it today.

Wright finally returned home in June of 1946 and was discharged

Loren holds a copy of a book about the Leopoldville *sinking.*

from the Army. His first order of business after his homecoming was to marry Joanna Williams, whom he had dated in high school. The two were joined in matrimony on July 21, 1946 in Coal City, Indiana. Soon the couple was raising their three children: Cheryl, Richard and Carla.

For the first several years, Wright worked with his father as a carpenter. He moved his family to Spencer, Indiana in 1950 and shortly after began a new job as a carpenter with Allison GM in 1951. He remained with Allison's for the next 32 years.

In the summer of 1963, Wright built a new home for his family in Mooresville, Indiana. He and his wife still live there today.

Wright retired from Allison's in 1983. But he has remained active with woodworking projects. He belongs to the International Wood Collectors Society.

Even though almost 70 years have passed since that fateful Christmas Eve in 1944, Wright still carries heartache over the tragedy on the English Channel. What

Loren with his great nephew, Chad Thatcher, in front of WWII Memorial.

bothers him most is the Department of Defense's long secrecy of the whereabouts of those comrades who died in the sinking of their ship.[2]

"That hurt me because I thought the government didn't treat our boys right", he said. "Their families, either. Many of them died long before the details of their loved ones' deaths became known."

There are some things which ease Wright's pain: faith in God, playing folk music on his guitar, spending time with his wife and family, working with wood.

Recently Wright had the opportunity to go to Washington D.C. to see the World War 2 Memorial. He was on the 5th Indy Honor Flight that left Indianapolis on May 10th, 2014 — exactly 70 years to the day of his entering the service on May 10, 1944. He even got to see and shake hands with former Senator Bob Dole who was at the Tomb of the Unknown Soldier.

The heartache from war remains. But the blessings in life are thankfully just a little stronger.

---

2 In 1984 the shipwreck organization NUMA, under the leadership of Clive Cussler, located the sunken *SS Leopold* off the coast of Cherbourg, France. She remains sunken at sea today.

NORTH AFRICA & CHINA-BURMA-INDIA THEATER

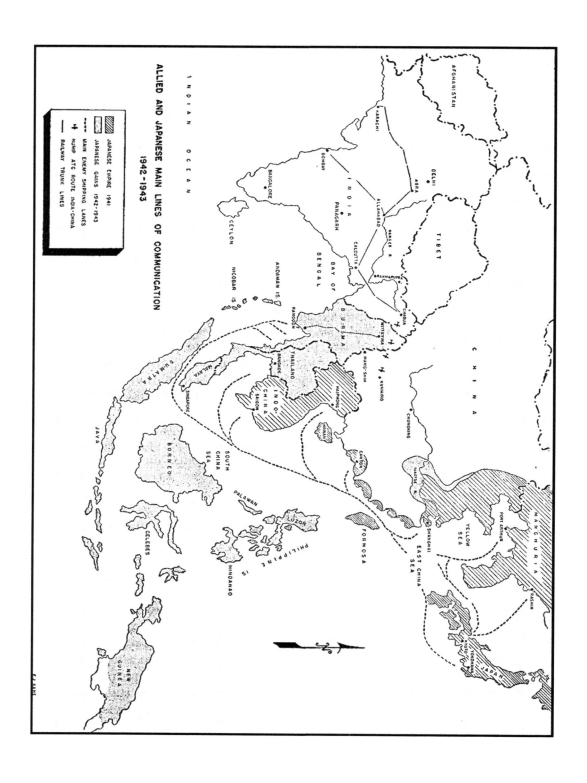

ALLIED AND JAPANESE MAIN LINES OF COMMUNICATION
1942 - 1943

A Craftsman for Life

Veteran was a Wood Warrior at Home and Abroad

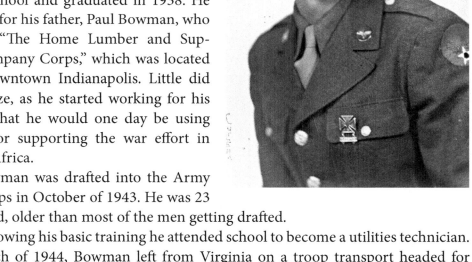

For most service members in World War II the weapons of choice were rifles, machine guns and bombs. David Bowman preferred different weapons — things like hammers, nails, screws and saws.

Born on August 25, 1920, the Indianapolis native attended Arsenal Tech High School and graduated in 1938. He worked for his father, Paul Bowman, who owned "The Home Lumber and Supply Company Corps," which was located near downtown Indianapolis. Little did he realize, as he started working for his father, that he would one day be using wood for supporting the war effort in North Africa.

Bowman was drafted into the Army Air Corps in October of 1943. He was 23 years old, older than most of the men getting drafted.

Following his basic training he attended school to become a utilities technician. In March of 1944, Bowman left from Virginia on a troop transport headed for North Africa. While crossing the Atlantic Ocean he cut the hair of the men on board ship to raise money, which he sent home to his first wife, Norma, whom he had married just before leaving for the service.

Bowman arrived in Africa and spent time serving at Hay Army Airfield in French Morocco. His unit helped build airstrips for the glider planes that were used in combat operations.

Communications tower 2.

A master craftsman with wood, Bowman was soon using his preferred 'weapons' to build portable latrine boxes, mess tables and other support items for forward operating bases. He even built wheelchairs for injured service members.

Most of the building blueprints used inches and feet measurements. But the materials he received were in metric units. He had to work through the conversion formulas.

His most important contribution was the design and construction of mobile telecommunication control towers used in setting up advance bases in combat zones. Bowman designed the towers to be erected by four men in just 1.5 hours.

Especially noteworthy was Bowman's ability to salvage parts from wrecked gliders to fully assemble and outfit the control towers. Once built, the towers were used to support the sophisticated high frequency direction finder equipment that guided planes to airfields.

His design for the pre-fabricated towers earned him the first of his three bronze stars and was even forwarded up to higher command for replication in other combat zones. His bronze star award write-up included the following narrative:

"When late in January 1945, there was an immediate need for a combat control tower, this individual designed, constructed and erected a satisfactory tower in limited time. Plans for this tower have been submitted to higher headquarters for further use in this theater of operations. All materials used in the construction of this tower were from salvage, including nuts, bolts, and lag screws. This tower can be constructed and erected by four men in one and one-half hour time. Entirely prefabricated, the tower speeds the installation of all communications equipment and is constructed to permit installation of very high frequency direction finder equipment."

Bowman also helped to build and move bamboo huts used as officer quarters. The construction was often done with the most rudimentary of equipment and materials. "We had to use crowbars to dig holes for setting the posts," he told his son, Matt.

On one occasion he came across a boa python while working. "I just about wet my pants," he said, recalling the frightening moment.

Not all of his time was spent on the ground building. Bowman also got to experience flying over the *'hump'* — a term the Allies used for the Himalayan Mountain Range. Flying over it was extremely dangerous as a result of the high elevation necessary for the planes to cross over the mountain range. Such elevation often produced violent turbulence, high wind speed, icing and inclement weather conditions. "I was scared to death," Bowman recalled of the dangerous flight! But he crossed it without incident.

During more pleasant travel, Bowman was able to see the Taj

**Bowman Holding Japanese Flag, top.
Items from Jap Zero, above.**

Mahal in Angra, India and even attend an event at which Mahatma Ghandi spoke.

When the war ended, Bowman was at an airfield in which a Japanese Zero had been parked. Recognizing a trophy opportunity, he quickly climbed into the cockpit and, with his tiny pocketknife, cut out the artificial horizon scope, bomb gauge, schematic and joystick to take home as spoils.

Bowman arrived back in the U.S. in late December of 1945, after having served 21 months overseas in a theater of combat. At the time of his discharge he had risen to the rank of Tech Sergeant.

David and wife, Kathleen.

He was reunited with his wife, Norma, and quickly set to work building that which would become most important to him — his family. Bowman and Norma raised three children: Lynn, Michael and Marilee. He later married a second wife, Kathleen, and with her raised another son, Matt.

Bowman was reactivated and served stateside another 8 months in 1951 in support of the Korean War.

Bowman spent his civilian career working at his father's lumber company in Indianapolis, eventually taking over the business along with his brother. Ever the craftsman, Bowman built a sturdy home for his family on Graceland Avenue in Indianapolis.

He operated the business until 1994 when it tragically burned down in a fire. He and son, Matt, then started another lumber company, from which Bowman retired in 2005 at the age of 85.

Bowman has been a proud member of the American Legion Post 145 in Avon, Indiana. He has participated in several community parades as well as the Blue Star Event.

Summarizing his father's lasting contribution, son Michael said, "He has been a hardworking, honest man who has always taken care of his family."

Today, 94-year-old David Bowman enjoys his easy chair and spending time with his family, which now includes grandchildren and great-grandchildren.

Bowman participating in the Veteran Parade.

Tap Warrior in the Orient
WWII Veteran Worked as Morse Code Operator

Most of the soldiers, marines or airman in World War II used their fingers to pull a trigger on a weapon or operate some big piece of equipment. Some men, however, used their fingers to tap out critical messages in support of the war effort. Keith Gabhart of Martinsville, Indiana was one of those "tap warriors."

Gabhart was a Morse code radio operator with the Army Air Corps. His "weapon" was a small electronic gadget with an oval dial for tapping. His ammunition was a series of dashes and dots that he produced using the tips of his fingers, the combination of which spelled out letters forming words.

Born in 1922 in Valley Mills, Indiana Gabhart left high school at the age of 17 and joined the Civilian Conservation Corps (CCC), the U.S. government's public work relief program for unemployed, unmarried men from relief families. The creation of the corps was part of Roosevelt's New Deal program to assign unemployed men to rural labor projects throughout the U.S. to assist with conservation of natural resources. Gabhart's mother didn't want him to join the CCC because his older brother, Paul had died in a vehicle accident at a CCC camp in Plymouth, Indiana. But Gabhart felt the tug and, in spite of his mom's objection, joined the corps. He was assigned to the CCC camp in Pinedale, Wyoming where he cut down trees and helped build roads around Lake Freemont. He served there for a year.

When he returned home, he knew that his chances were high for being drafted. So he decided to enlist instead in the Army Air Corps. He was sworn in at Fort Benjamin Harrison in Indianapolis on August 19th, 1942. Two weeks after he enlisted, his draft notice arrived in the mail.

After spending a week in Atlantic City, New Jersey (marching on the famed boardwalk), he was sent to basic training at Scott Field in Bellville, Illinois. Following his graduation from boot camp he went to Smokey Hill Army Airfield near Salina, Kansas for three to four months of special training as a Morse code radio operator.

Morse code is an alphabetic code of long and short sounds, originally transmitted by telegraph. Each letter in the alphabet has a corresponding sound or series of sounds unique to it. The long sounds are referred to as dashes, while the short sounds are dots. Varying lengths of silence denote spaces between letters or words.

To make a dot on a telegraph, the telegraph key or switch was depressed and allowed to rapidly spring back. To make a dash the key was held down longer before allowing it to rebound. Thus messages were sent by tapping the key in a rhythm of coded letters. Messages were received via a radio transceiver, sounding like dots and dashes of static. (Wikipedia)

Morse Code Chart

A ● ▬	J ● ▬ ▬ ▬	S ● ● ●
B ▬ ● ● ●	K ▬ ● ▬	T ▬
C ▬ ● ▬ ●	L ● ▬ ● ●	U ● ● ▬
D ▬ ● ●	M ▬ ▬	V ● ● ● ▬
E ●	N ▬ ●	W ● ▬ ▬
F ● ● ▬ ●	O ▬ ▬ ▬	X ▬ ● ● ▬
G ▬ ▬ ●	P ● ▬ ▬ ●	Y ▬ ● ▬ ▬
H ● ● ● ●	Q ▬ ▬ ● ▬	Z ▬ ▬ ● ●
I ● ●	R ● ▬ ●	

Gabhart's training was intensive! "The required minimum rate was 16 words per minute," Gabhart recalled. Operators who were unable to reach that average failed the program. Gabhart excelled to a speedy average of 25 words a minute!

Had there been cell phones with texting features back then, Gabhart would no doubt have competed with the most proficient teen texter in tapping on letter keys to form words.

Upon the completion of his training in Kansas, Gabhart was assigned to the 20th Air Force, 58th Bombardment Wing, 468th Bomb Group, 793rd Squadron.

In February 1944, the 468th Bomb Group left Kansas for Kalaikunda Air Base near Kharagpur, India. The Group's mission was to support flight operations in the China-Burma-India theatre. Gabhart tapped his Morse code messages into China and across the South Pacific.

Following his 6 months in India, Gabhart was transferred to the Chengtu Area Airfields in China, where he spent another 6 months. His final duty location was on Tinian Island. The power for sending Morse code came from diesel engine generators, as there was no electricity where he served in China or Tinian.

Much of Gabhart's Morse code communication was relaying messages to large air bases in China and India. One of the most important communications Gabhart had was with radio operators on Allied war planes. There were times that pilots would get lost in the air and need assistance with getting back to home base. Gabhart had direction finding equipment that he used to pinpoint the location of the lost plane. Then, through Morse code messaging, he sent directions to the radio operator on the plane (whose training included interpreting Morse code) who then conveyed the information to the plane's navigator.

In 1994, by happenstance, Gabhart spoke by phone with one of the pilots whose B-29 crew he helped save 50 years earlier. It was August of 1944 and Gabhart was serving in China. On August 20th a B-29 bombing mission left Western China to bomb a steel mill in Yawata, Japan. During the return flight back to base one of the B-29's radioed the airbase in China requesting navigational assistance via the base's direction finding equipment. But the base wasn't responding to any of the attempted radio con-

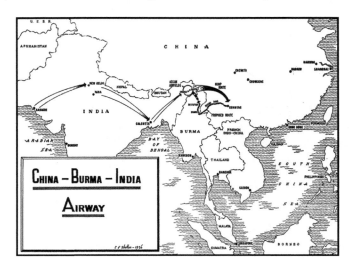

Gabhart's Morse code transmitter mounted on a piece of wood.

tacts. The radioman on the plane heard some communication from other planes being received at the Allied airbase in India, 1,800 miles away. So, he made contact with India and requested assistance. The India base sent the direction finding requests to the China base via Morse code and, after receiving the navigational information, relayed it back to the B-29 planes flying over China. The vital information helped to save a dozen or so planes and crews from possibly getting lost and having to crash land.

After safely landing in China, the pilot of the plane learned why there was a problem making radio contact with the China base. The long-range high frequency signals from the plane were skipping over the base, preventing the radio communication from being received. The radio signals were, however, able to reach the India base. So, the requests were relayed from India to China and then back to India for transmitting the information to the planes needing it.

It turned out that Gabhart was the ground station Morse Code Radio Operator at the China base the evening of August 20th. He provided the critical communication link between the radio operator in India and the Direction Finder operator in China. He recalled of that evening, "We knew we should be hearing from a lot of planes but weren't, and until India asked us to provide a DF (Direction Finder) steer on a B-29 over Eastern China, we didn't realize calls to us were skipping over us. I received India's request (via Morse Code) and yelled it across the Radio Room to the DF Operator who took a bearing on the signal and yelled the bearing back to me for relay to India. I have forgotten how many crews we helped that night, but we were busy for several hours after that first call." There were at least 11 other B-29 crews that had requested navigation assistance and received it via the India-China-India relay.

It's difficult to know how many planes and crews may have been saved from disaster through Gabhart's tapping fingers during his 18 months in the China-Burma-India Theater!

Gabhart's squadron was on the island of Tinian when the Japanese surrendered and the war came to an end. It was from Tinian that the B-29 bomber, "Bockscar" left on August 9th, 1945 to drop the atomic bomb on Nagasaki.

Gabhart was honorably discharged from the 1505th Army Air Force base at Patterson Field near Dayton, Ohio on October 23, 1945. He left the Army Air Corps as a Sergeant, having served for three years and having earned a Distinguished Unit Badge, a Good Conduct Medal and an Asiatic-Pacific Theater Ribbon w/one silver star and one bronze star.

He hitchhiked from Dayton back home to Indiana where he started the next chapter of his life.

Gabhart married his wife, Allien in 1952, and together they raised a family of four children: Phillip Dale "Buddy" Gabhart , Steven Kent "Stevie" Cochran; Helen Hayes and Linda Jane Rodgers.

Gabhart re-enlisted during the Korean War in the early 1950s.

Following his war service, Gabhart worked as a nickel-chrome plater, as a bottled gas deliveryman for Philips Petroleum Company and later as a self-employed public accountant in the Indianapolis area.

In his spare time he enjoyed playing guitar, singing and most importantly his family. He took great delight in constructing trails in the woods and taking his grandchildren on wagon rides with his John Deere tractor.

Gabhart died on September 20, 2013 at the age of 90. Although it had been close to seven decades since he used Morse code in the war, even in his later years he could still tap out each letter from memory. He even taught his children, grandchildren and great-grandchildren how to do it.

468th Bombardment Group Martin-Omaha B-29-25-MO Superfortress 42-65276. 793d Bombardment squadron, Kharagpur Airfield, India.

B-29-1-BA Superfortress of the 468th bomb group 793rd BS, "Lassie" nose art, CBI 1944-1945.

Flying Low in Burma

Small plane pilot flew medical evacuation missions

World War II battles encompassed half of the globe. The battle sites that most people remember are in Europe or the Islands of the South Pacific. But the China-Burma-India Theater was another significant combat location as well. Just ask Jerry Morehead of Morgan County, Indiana. He flew small planes on medical evacuation missions in Burma.

Morehead, a Mooresville, Indiana resident, had joined the Indiana National Guard while still a student at Washington High School. He was assigned to the 38th Division, HQ Company.

Following graduation he began his basic training. He spent 9 months at Camp Shelby in Mississippi, where he was put in charge of the National Guard Base Post Office.

Three months following the attack on Pearl Harbor, Morehead decided to pursue becoming a pilot. He applied for pilot training with the Army Air Forces and started his pre-flight training at Kelly Field in San Antonio, Texas. His efforts stalled at flight training when he had difficulty performing the required spins on the aircraft.

Although he washed out of flight school and never flew the big planes, Morehead was given permission to fly some small planes that were being used in the China-Burma-India Theater of operations. There was a critical need there for pilots to fly small planes for medical evacuation and rescue missions. The small planes were used for evacuations because of their capacity to land almost anywhere — roads, sand bars, level ground, sand and even rice paddies. Morehead was just the man for the job.

He was attached to a unit of 500 pilots flying British and American planes, including Gliders, L-5, L-1 and Piper Cub aircraft. He arrived in Karachi, India and began his flight missions. "My job was to fly the specially fitted Piper Cubs (small planes) to pick up wounded and injured soldiers along the Burma Road and in the jungle fighting areas," he recalled.

The Burma Road was the critical transportation link allowing the flow of supplies to China. When the Japanese overran Burma in 1942, the road was shut down to Allied supply runs. British and American forces finally defeated the Japanese in Northern Burma. The Ledo Road was built and connected to the Burma Road. By January of 1945, Allied trucks were finally able to drive all the way to China.

The Piper Cubs were small but could transport up to eleven injured soldiers. After picking up the injured men Morehead and the other pilots transported them to the surgical Army units in Myitkyina, Burma, where over one hundred operations were performed each day by Army surgeons.

Japanese forces were located just a few miles from the surgery tent. "You could see the Japs cooking breakfast," Morehead recalled of his view from the air.

Some of the medical evacuees that Morehead transported were part of "Merrill's Marauders"- the famous Army special operations jungle warfare unit that fought the Japanese deep in the jungles along the China-Burma-India corridor.

Morehead remembered several close calls with his flying. On one occasion he was transporting boxes of dynamite to be used in blowing up trees so that dirt runways could be built. On another occasion he recalled taking off from a rugged field runway that was cut into the side of a mountain. He dropped 10 feet while beginning his lift off, but fortunately the trees had been cut down so that he didn't crash.

All of Morehead's missions were dangerous. His plane was not equipped with a radio. So, if he ever had mechanical trouble and had to land somewhere else, he couldn't communicate his whereabouts. He was flying over enemy territory and taking off and landing on tricky cleared jungle runways.

The Piper Cub planes were also quite slow and no match for the Japanese Zero fighter planes. Morehead somehow avoided detection by any Zero pilots.

He did not, however, avoid detection from the Japanese guns on the ground. Morehead recalled, "Since we had to fly low when flying our missions, the Japanese would often shoot at us with their rifles and machine guns." Only one bullet ever penetrated Morehead's plane.

Other pilots were not as fortunate as Morehead. He recalled that over 600 planes and over 1,000 men on flights carrying supplies to China were lost. Morehead remembered the somber task of flying his Piper Cub in search of lost planes.

Although he was never shot down, Morehead did sustain serious injury. On his last mission he was approaching the airfield for a landing in Missional, Burma. Another plane was coming in as well. Morehead had no clear landing instructions. In an effort to

Morehead in body cast.

avoid colliding with the other plane, he was forced to do a nosedive crash on the runway. His passenger escaped injury, but Morehead broke his back in the emergency crash landing.

He was taken to a hospital in Ledo, India where he spent the next two months recovering in a full-body cast. The back pain and uncomfortable body cast were not his only challenges there. Heat and humidity plagued him as well. He recalled, "I remember it being so hot, over 100 degrees, and there was only one fan in the hospital. Luckily for me, it was beside my bed."

Morehead's spirits were lifted considerably when he received a surprise visit from Gordon, one of his best friends from high school. They had joined the service together but had been separated after their initial assignments. Gordon, who was stationed in Calcutta, had learned of Morehead's hospitalization in Ledo in a letter

Jerry and his wife, Lorraine.

from his mother and had hitchhiked on a plane and flew 600 miles just to visit him. "Now that's friendship," Morehead exclaimed!

In September of 1944, Morehead was sent to Billings Hospital at Fort Benjamin Harrison, Indiana where he completed his recovery.

Morehead was discharged as a Tech Sergeant in August of 1945 in Ardmore, Oklahoma after having served for 3 years and 6 months.

Following his discharge he returned to Indianapolis, Indiana. He took a course in selling insurance and made a career of it. Later in life he worked at the Industrial and Automotive Hardware, where he was a manager and salesman. He didn't retire until he was 88!

Morehead and his wife, Lorraine, celebrated their 50th wedding anniversary in 2013.

Morehead's most recent flight was on a charter to Washington D.C. in April of 2013. He was one of the 70 veterans who were flown free of charge by Indy Honor Flight to see the World War II Memorial erected in his honor.

PACIFIC THEATER

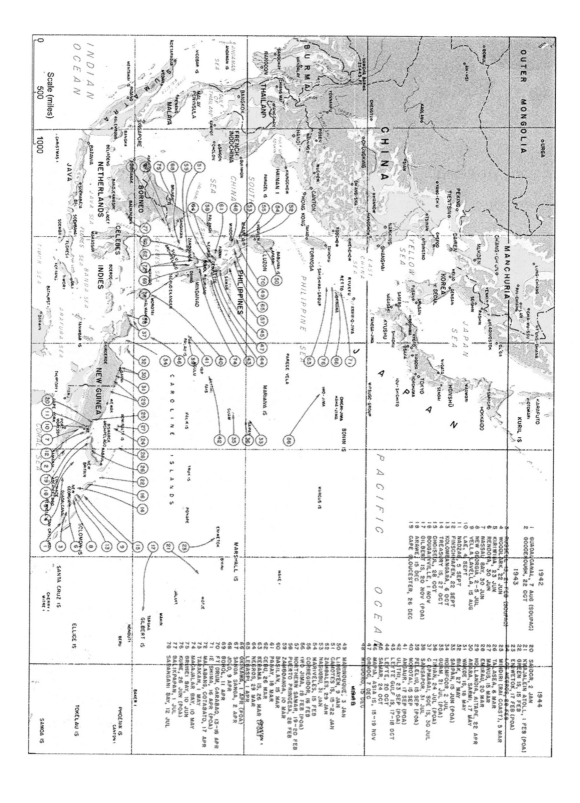

Dirty Duty on an Aircraft Carrier
Sailor Served On Famed USS Enterprise *(CV-6)*

Arthur Brown knew a thing or two about surviving battles at sea during World War II. The rural Morgantown, Indiana resident lived through plenty of them while serving as a ship fitter responsible for damage control and firefighting aboard the famed U.S. Navy aircraft carrier, *USS Enterprise* (CV-6).

Spared from the attack on Pearl Harbor because of a delay in returning from Wake Island, the *Enterprise* quickly entered the war in the Pacific. She took part in the Battle of Midway in June 1942 before returning to Pearl Harbor for a month of rest and replenishment. It was during her rest in Pearl Harbor that Seaman Arthur Brown, fresh from his rushed two weeks of Boot Camp in San Diego, reported aboard.

Brown, who was from Fort Dodge, Iowa and one of five from his family to serve in the war, explained his rationale for enlisting: "Well, if they're (his brothers) going, I'm going." And as to his choice of the Navy, he recalled saying to the recruiter, "I don't know how to dig a foxhole, but I know how to swim, so I'll go with the Navy."

Brown was assigned to the R Division of ship fitters on the *Enterprise*. Ship fitters built and repaired the structural parts of the ship. In addition to ship fitting, Brown had the collateral duty of being on the damage control team. Having gone through an accelerated boot camp, he had to learn his trade of damage control and firefighting on the go while the ship left Hawaii and headed back to the South Pacific for combat duty. "We put the fires out," Brown said. "Any plumbing went

Arthur (middle) and his siblings in uniform.

to heck or something down in the galley had to be fixed or down there where the doctors operate and everything…we had to go down there and plug stuff. We worked all over the ship."

In fact, ship fitters not only worked all over the ship, they also lived all over the ship. As Brown explained, "You couldn't put 'em all in one group, not when you were in battle and you got blown up; because you couldn't lose all them men at one time. So they split us up."

Arthur (3rd from right) with shipfitters on *Enterprise's* deck.

Brown and the other crew members assigned to damage control got plenty of opportunity to hone their skills in putting out fires, plugging holes in the hull and making critical repairs. The *Enterprise* was under frequent attack from Japanese planes, ships and submarines and was hit on numerous occasions. She was kept afloat only through the efforts of her dedicated crew.

Burial at sea.

The hardest part of Brown's job was gathering the bodies of the injured and dying after a battle. In the aftermath of explosions men would be trapped inside the ship's compartments and needed to be freed from the airtight spaces. Many of them would be severely injured and some of them already dead. "If they were still alive, we would send them over to the hospital ship," Brown said. "If they weren't, we'd put five-inch projectiles between their legs and 40 millimeters on their arms, wrap them up like a mummy and just throw them over the side for sea burial." It was nothing to lose 50-60 men if the ship was hit with a 500 lb. bomb. "We got blown up a lot of times," Brown recalled. "We had a dirty job!"

Brown's earliest experiences of combat at sea came in late 1942. "We went down there to Guadalcanal, Espiritu Santo in the New Hebrides," he said. "We used that for our home port. We operated out of there. Every night we had Jap planes fly over. We called them, 'sewing machine charley.' They'd come fly over there every night. Sometimes the Japs would drop a bomb and sometimes they wouldn't, but they kept us on our toes at night. So, our ship was in 'Condition 2' regardless, all the time." (Condition 2 described the ships state of combat readiness. In condition 2 half the guns were manned.)

Bomb hits near USS Enterprise during Battle of Sana Cruz Islands.

Pilot of a Japanese dive bomber about to crash his "Val" into Hornet's signal bridge.

Brown also witnessed the sinking of other ships in his task force. He recalled of the Battle of Santa Cruz, "They (the Japanese) were bombing Guadalcanal all the time we were there. When the Hornet (another aircraft carrier) got sunk, we were the only carrier left in the Pacific. I saw her sink." (Hornet was sunk on October 26, 1942.)

The *Enterprise* was also damaged during the same battle. Brown remembered, "It was both decks. We got hit in compartment A306, and it blew all that out up there. You take a 500 pound bomb!..." At the time of the strikes, Brown was serving as a phone talker in A310, which was right over the central station.

It was clear that the *Enterprise* was going to need some extensive repairs. She departed for New Caledonia. But even before she had been completely repaired, the *Enterprise* was called back out to Guadalcanal for combat duty in November of 1942.

Brown recalled the urgency for the *Enterprise's* return to Guadalcanal: "We went right back out to the Solomon Islands. The Japanese were going to take Guadalcanal back over at the time, and they had about 10 or 12 transports loaded with troops. They had more people on those ships than

USS Enterprise.

we had troops on the island, and they were going to take over Guadalcanal."

The battle plan that was drawn up involved deception and the use of *Enterprise* as a decoy. Brown explained: "We came from the south and the Japs were coming in here with these transports, loaded down to take over the island again. So, we launched our aircraft off our ship to Guadalcanal — fighter planes and dive bombers, torpedo planes and everything else."

Photographed immediately after a prelanding strike by USS Enterprise aircraft flown by Navy pilots, Tanambogo and Gavutu Islands lie smoking and in ruins.

After the surprise launch of the aircraft, *Enterprise* went into the decoy mode. Brown recalled thinking, "We are being used as a decoy. That was the way it looked to me. We were coming around the island to launch our stuff, and here comes the Japs. So, we took off. We were 'hauling ass.' That ship was shaking! We were doing 36 knots. The Japs detached the warships that were escorting their transports. They came after us. Well they couldn't catch us 'cause we were moving fast. I mean, that's the way it was set up. While they were chasing us, our aircraft off Guadalcanal sunk every one of those (transport) ships. And they figured they killed at least from 12,000–15,000 troops on the ships.'"

In a twist of irony, 'Tokyo Rose' had earlier reported that the *Enterprise* had been sunk. So, thinking that another U.S. ship was ripe for sinking, the Japanese warships had taken off after her, only to discover in dismay that the *Enterprise* was alive and well. And worse yet, she had already launched her aircraft, which were at that moment exacting their damage on the Japanese transport ships that the warships had left unprotected. Sixteen Japanese ships would be sunk and eight others damaged. The decoy had worked. And the island of Guadalcanal had been spared from the fresh assault of more Japanese troops.

Following the Battle at Guadalcanal, the *Enterprise* returned to Noumea for repairs. Once fixed, she trained out of Espiritu Santo in the New Hebrides and provided support for U.S. surface forces up to the Solomon Islands.

Arthur, second from right, and buddies.

While most of the time his experience in the South Pacific was serious and intense, there were moments of humor for Brown and his buddies. One such moment had to do with witnessing a jeep being stolen. The *Enterprise*, like other aircraft carriers, had begun using military jeeps (called jeep spotters) to help tow aircraft into position on the deck. At one point, the jeep on *Enterprise* became inoperable. While the carrier was at Espirtu Santo, Brown and some of his buddies were on shore off-duty. They were having some beers when they saw a new jeep pull up to the island post office.

As Brown recalled, "One of the orderlies came up there and he had all that gold on, you know, never had a spot of dirt on his clothes. He drove a jeep that was brand new. It shined like a brand new penny. Boy, I mean it was shiny! Meantime, *Enterprise's* aviation mechanics — the airstrip was just a little ways and they walked down there to drink beer with us — they spotted that jeep. They stole it, put it on the barge and took it to our ship. You ain't seen nothing until you've seen this guy come out with two arms full of mail looking for his jeep. And we had it! It's a wonder we didn't die laughing. So, our mechanics stripped it down and made a plane spotter out of it on the ship."

By the early summer of 1943, other aircraft carriers arrived in the South Pacific, allowing the *Enterprise* to return to the U.S. for an important refit. On her trip back to the States, she stopped briefly at Pearl Harbor where she received the Presidential Unit citation from Admiral Chester Nimitz. The carrier arrived at the Puget Sound Naval Shipyard on July 20, 1943. For the next few months, she received some important upgrades.

Enterprise was back in the South Pacific by November of 1943. In mid-February of 1944, *Enterprise* (still with Task Force 58) attacked the Japanese Naval Base at Truk

Lagoon, located in the chain of Caroline Islands. Brown recalled, "They dropped flares on us out there and I saw one plane come down right by our tower on the ship — you know, we're up about fifty feet off the water. Anyway, we got a lot of our men hurt. We got caught in a cross-fire from our own escort ships. Anybody on the flight deck — gunners and stuff like that — shrapnel got 'em. It was awful!"

USS Enterprise, 1944.

Brown's perch on deck afforded him another view — that of the Japanese ships being hit by the U.S. planes as they tried to escape from the base. He recalled, "When the Jap (ships) came out of there (the base), we would detach our battleships or cruisers. I could see them shooting at those ships over there. I could see 'em smoking to beat the band and, just like you took a knife and cut it, sink them. I could see it, just like watching television off the ship."

In June of 1944, the *USS Enterprise* took part in supporting the Allied Invasions of Saipan, Rota and Guam — all part of the Marianas Island chain. It was during the invasion of Saipan that Brown got his closest look at an island under Allied attack. He watched as the cruisers and battleships from the *Enterprise* task force fired on the island. "They detached our cruisers and battleships and fired broadside up the side of the mountain," he recalled.

"It was the first time we'd ever seen them fire a 16-inch gun. You know how you can fire a pistol. It's instantaneous, you know. Bang! It's right there. And I watched them fire them 16s. Boom! You know, boom! I thought, 'Well, it will be over with before I get a chance to turn around.' But it didn't happen that way. I waited and waited and

Loading bomb on SBD aboard *USS Enterprise*, Aug. 7, 1944.

16-inch guns on *USS Enterprise*.

waited, and thought, 'Well, hell, it ain't gonna work. Must be a dud or something!' Then I looked up and it blew up. It took a long time for that shell to get from the ship to the island."

The 16-inch projectiles weren't the only things hitting the island. The task force was also firing napalm at the enemy bombardments. Napalm was developed in 1943, and was used as an incendiary device against the Japanese during some of the island campaigns, as well as against mainland Japan. Brown recalled that it was powerful and dangerous stuff. "They mixed them — I call them jelly bombs — fire bombs. They mixed them on the stern of our ship and put it on the fighters. Those fighters would go in. The pilots behind would take pictures of the guy ahead of him when he dropped and released it. It would disintegrate anything. They showed us some of it on the ship. They mixed it on the stern fantail, and it scared me. I'd always go to the other end. All I know, it was awful! It wouldn't have done any good — I don't care where you went on the ship — if it went up, you know. But I always went to the other end, got the hell away."

"The fighters would go in just above treetop, see, and when they got to the mountains where the Japanese were dug in, they would release them jelly bombs, and they'd just destroy everything. I mean, I don't care what the hell it was, just destroy it!"

It was while chasing the Japanese toward mainland Japan that the crew of the *Enterprise* came up against one of their most violent foes ever — a typhoon. Brown recalled: "You can't believe … I'd never seen this before. I don't know how we stayed afloat. I could look up from the hangar deck or wherever I was and see our other ships. Then big swells would come up. The stern would be out of the water and then the bow would be out of the water. They'd come up on one of them big swells and they'd just drop down and disappear. We had waves come up to the flight deck. It's about 50 foot off the water. How it stayed afloat, I'll never know!"

While supporting the invasion of Okinawa during March-May of 1945, the *USS Enterprise,* along with the other Allied ships, came under heavy attack from Kamikazes. On two different occasions kamikaze pilots hit the *Enterprise*, resulting in damage to the ship and tragic loss of life for some of the crew.

Recalling the attacks Brown said, "If you saw them (the Zeroes), it scared the hell out of you, because I don't care where you were at on the ship, when they came out of the sun you'd swear they were coming right at you and nobody else. You're the only one on that ship when you look up there. 'Well, my ass done had it!' you thought. That's the way it felt."

A photo taken from the battleship *Washington* shows an explosion on *Enterprise* from a bomb-laden kamikaze. The ship's forward elevator was blown approximately 400 feet (120 m) into the air from the force of the explosion six decks below.

Brown's "dirty job" in combat lasted for 28 straight months. Just before the 2nd kamikaze attack on the *USS Enterprise* in May of 1945, his combat tour came to an end as he received orders for shore duty. He got his ride back stateside from

Firefighting on *USS Enterprise* following a Kamikaze attack.

Brown with a framed photograph of the explosion aboard the USS Enterprise *after the kamikaze attack.*

Pearl Harbor on the USS Bunker Hill, the same aircraft carrier he had witnessed getting hit by a kamikaze while back at Okinawa.

The dropping of the atomic bombs on Hiroshima (August 6, 1945) and Nagasaki (August 9, 1945) forced the surrender of the Japanese and brought an end to World War II. By the end of the war the *USS Enterprise* became the most decorated ship of World War II, having earned 20 battle stars. At one point in the war, the *Enterprise* was the only operating carrier in the Pacific for 10 months. She was involved in all but two of the twenty major naval battles in the Pacific, and Arthur Brown was on board the ship for all but one of those 18 battles!

At the end of the war, Brown was honorably discharged and returned home to Iowa. He married Elizabeth Rowena Lepley and later moved to Indiana where he worked for Martin Marietta in Indianapolis, as the head of maintenance until retiring in 1992. Brown and his wife raised three children: Arthur Jr., Kathleen, and Carl. He was father to a fourth child, Steven Wayne.

Brown married his second wife, Dorothy Jean Conway, on August 23, 1969.

In retirement, he remained active in the welding trade, handcrafting unique pieces of welding art, many of which were displayed in his home in Brown County, Indiana.

In his later years, Brown became more active in sharing his service story with others.

In November of 2009, the American Legion of Brown County presented Brown with a complete set of replacement medals in a display case during a special ceremony. Brown had never received his medals after being discharged from the Navy.

Brown with the replacement medals he finally received in November of 2009.

In July of 2011, he took part in the last National *USS Enterprise* Reunion, which was held in Austin, TX. His photograph and some of his quotes from an interview appeared in an article published in the Austin American Statesman newspaper.

In 2012, Brown got the privilege of attending the deactivation ceremony for the *USS Enterprise* CV65 in Norfolk, VA. He not only climbed up all the stairs to the top of the bridge to sit in the captain's chair, he also had a private visit with the Commanding Officer, Capt. Bill Hamilton, who presented him with a medallion commemorating the ship's 51st anniversary. Brown's photograph from that visit appeared for a time on the U.S. Navy's website.

Brown died on July 28, 2013 at the age of 90. He was buried near his home at East Hill Cemetery in Morgantown, IN.

More on the USS Enterprise

The *USS Enterprise* was awarded a Presidential Unit Citation for her service during World War II. The citation states:

> "For consistently outstanding performance and distinguished achievement during repeated action against enemy Japanese forces in the Pacific war area, 7 December 1941, to 15 November 1942. Participating in nearly every major carrier engagement in the first year of the war, the Enterprise and her air group, exclusive of far-flung destruction of hostile shore installations throughout the battle area, did sink or damage on her own a total of 35 Japanese vessels and shot down a total of 185 Japanese aircraft. Her aggressive spirit and superb combat efficiency are fitting tribute to the officers and men who so gallantly established her as an ahead bulwark in the defense of the American nation."

In addition to her Presidential Unit Citation, Enterprise received the Navy Unit Commendation and 20 battle stars for World War II service, making her the highest decorated US ship ever.

Finally, she was presented with a British Admiralty Pennant that was hoisted when a majority of the Admiralty Board members were present. The pennant was given to the "Big E" as a token of respect from an ally. Enterprise is the only ship outside the Royal Navy to receive the honor in the more than 400 years since its creation.

Enterprise was inactivated on 1 December 2012 at Norfolk Naval Station, Virginia. Naval enthusiasts have requested that she be converted into a museum. In 2012, the United States Department of Defense deemed this too expensive. What remains of *Enterprise* in 2015 is currently scheduled to be taken to Washington state for scrapping, though it remains possible the ship's island could be removed and used as a memorial. She has been towed to Newport News Shipyard for continued dismantling.

USS Enterprise *(CVN-65) dismantling,*
December 2014.

Sponsors for Art's Story

MEREDITH-CLARK FUNERAL HOME

The Brown family chose Meredith-Clark Funeral Home in Morganstown to handle all the arrangements for Art's cremation, visitation and burial.

At Meredith-Clark Funeral Home we pride ourselves in being "Family Owned" and residents of the community. We have been in business since 1935, and from the beginning our commitment to you, your family and the community has been important to us. We are sensitive to your needs from the first phone call until long after the funeral is over.

At Meredith-Clark Funeral Home we can help you plan a service so special that the only thing you leave behind are beautiful memories. When a family entrusts us with their loved ones, they can rest assured that all is cared for with dignity and respect.

Please call us at 812-597-4670 or find us on our website at: www.meredith-clark.com. Bill Meredith & Jamie Meredith, Owners

AMERICAN LEGION — NASHVILLE, IN POST # 13

The American Legion was chartered and incorporated by Congress in 1919 as a patriotic veterans organization devoted to mutual helpfulness. It is the nation's largest veterans' service organization, committed to mentoring and sponsorship of youth programs in our communities, advocating patriotism and honor,

Brown County Indiana Veterans Hall
902 Deer Run Lane • Nashville, IN

promoting a strong national security, and continued devotion to our fellow service members and veterans.

143

American Legion Post #13 is the local post in Nashville, Indiana. Art was a member of this post. The post learned that Art had never received his military medals after leaving the Navy. In 2009, at a special ceremony, the post presented Art with a set of his military medals displayed in a special glass case. Contact Nashville's American Legion Post at (812) 988-5600 or by email: <u>bcvet@att.net</u>.

World War II Memorial Park in Avon, IN.   PHOTO BY KARLIE ANN MAY

Getting a Closer Look
Veteran Watched for Enemy Aircraft in the South Pacific

William Davee was trained by the U.S. Army to use radar equipment and searchlights to get a closer look at enemy aircraft. By war's end he needed neither radar nor spotlight to track the enemy. The enemy was right in front of him!

Born on August 9, 1922 in Mahalasville, Indiana, Davee was the middle of eight children raised by his parents, Roy and Sadie Davee. He attended Morgantown High School through his freshman year and then quit to work on the family farm.

Davee was drafted into the Army in 1942, but he received a 6-month deferral so that he could help bring in the harvest before departing for military service.

Reporting to Ft. Bliss in El Paso, Texas for his basic training, Davee remained there for one year while completing his training on radar equipment and searchlights. Germany had already been using radar to detect enemy planes for some time. The Allies needed the same capability.

Davee recalled that his training on radar was often at night and sometimes lasted all night long.

Following his training he was assigned to the 233rd Searchlight Battalion, an Army Anti-Aircraft unit designed to search for, locate and destroy enemy aircraft.

Soldiers using a searchlight.

On August 9, 1943, the day of his 21st birthday, Davee and his unit left San Francisco on a ship that was headed to the South Pacific.

For the next two years Davee lived on four different islands. After spending a couple of months in Fiji to acclimatize to the weather and culture, his unit arrived in British Samoa. Japanese forces were never far from the island. The U.S. Marines kept it under guard to thwart any attack. Davee's unit spent a year there testing their radar equipment. "We could detect an airplane 100 miles away," he said in reference to the powerful equipment. "We could tell its distance, speed, elevation and identity."

In early 1945, the 233rd Searchlight Battalion moved to Guadalcanal. By this time Davee, who operated the power plant for the radar station, had become a Sergeant and was responsible for leading 21 guys. Along with the rest of the men, he took his turn on radar watches to identify incoming aircraft.

He recalled one occasional enemy that equally affected both the Japanese and the Allies — fog. When fog settled over the island it prevented the planes and ships from delivering the needed supplies to the U.S. forces. But it also prevented the Japanese from bombing Allied ships and planes.

The primary mission on Guadalcanal was for the Searchlight Battalion to test a searchlight system that was placed on a barge and floated out near an island. The goal was to be able to light up the beaches during an attack or amphibious landing. Tragically, Japanese forces killed most of the Marine riflemen who were operating the floating barge. Davee's unit was the next in line to run tests on the barge.

The unit had hardly settled at Guadalcanal when they were forced back to Fiji for a quarantine and medical observation. Although Davee escaped contracting malaria, others in his unit did not fare as well. During his time on Fiji, Davee and some comrades did manage to play some baseball, as a ball diamond had been laid out by earlier forces.

The battalion's next stop was on the island of New Guinea. Davee speculated that the unit remained there for about 6 months. Most of the time was spent maintaining their radar equipment and trailers.

Davee did recall a humorous incident while on the island. There was a large coconut grove there. When the ship carrying Davee's battalion first arrived on the island the native children came up to the men and sold them coconuts for $1. "It was good milk," Davee remembered. "But you don't want to drink too much of it or it will keep you going!" After Davee's unit settled on the island they found the coconut grove and became adept at harvesting their own fruit. "The kids sure made some money that first day," Davee said with a smile.

Six months later Davee and his unit found themselves in the Philippine Islands at Northern Luzon preparing with thousands of other troops for the anticipated invasion of Japan. "We received new equipment, clothing and boots," he said. But the new gear also sent a somber signal to the men. "It was pretty solemn," Davee recalled of the men's mood. "Everyone realized what was going to happen." He added, "They (the Japanese) were ready for war!"

Then suddenly things changed! In early August of 1945, while listening to an Australian radio station, Davee heard of Japan's surrender. "We had heard about some bombs being dropped the day before," Davee remarked. "But there was not much information on the power of effects of the bombs. But the next morning, the war was over! Everyone went running around in different directions in celebration!"

In one triumphant moment he was suddenly done with focusing on the enemy ... or so he thought.

Not having enough points to be sent home, Davee volunteered along with his friend, Sullivan, to guard a POW outpost in Baguio for the next several months. The outpost, which was used as a transfer station for captured Japanese soldiers, consisted of a few bamboo buildings designed to house 500 prisoners of war.

Each evening allied trucks would bring loads of Japanese soldiers who had been caught or surrendered.

Davee and Sullivan got a close look at all of them. The two men took turns doing 24-hour shifts to process the prisoners. "We made them take their clothes off and put things out in front of them," he explained. "We went through everything to make sure they had no weapons. We found swords, shells and grenades," he said.

Bamboo quarters.

Japanese soldiers reporting to POW camp.

"They shook like a leaf," Davee recalled of the Japanese soldiers. "They thought we were going to kill them." He added, "I guess any of us would have done the same if we were prisoners."

Far from killing them, Davee and Sullivan treated them humanely. They fed them, housed them and then sent them on to Manila in the Philippines for the next stop in the repatriation pipeline.

By late November of 1945, Davee was on his way back to U.S. soil for his discharge. But it was a rough ride home. Before boarding the cargo ship that was to take them home, the captain of the ship asked the men which route they wanted to take. The northern route was shorter in distance but rougher seas. The southern route was longer in distance but had calmer seas. Wanting to get home as fast as

Loading Japanese POWs.

possible, the soldiers chose the shorter route. "We didn't think about a bad storm," said Davee. "We just wanted to get home."

Most of them would regret that choice when their ship encountered a harsh storm that lasted for three days near the Aleutian Islands. "It was questionable if we were going to make it," Davee remembered. "The storm even scared the crew on the ship who thought this was one of the worst storms ever." The ship was in danger of going down as it was tossed around the huge swells. "If the ship had rolled another 5 degrees it would have capsized," Davee recalled.

Following their rough ride across the Pacific Ocean the ship finally reached the port of San Francisco on Christmas Eve of 1945. After being overseas for more than two years Davee was finally back on American soil.

He made his way home to Indiana. And one of his first orders of business was seeing Ms. Thelma Marie Robinson, whom he had begun dating before leaving for the war. "She sent me a letter every day," Davee said. He rewarded her for her diligent letter writing with a wedding ring.

The couple married on June 8, 1946. Their marriage was blessed with two children: Randy (1955) and Janice (1958). The couple went on to enjoy 67 years together before Thelma's death in June 2013.

When Davee wasn't focusing on family he was focusing on land — farm land to be exact. He and his brother purchased 475 acres off Mann Road (southwest of Indianapolis) in 1949. They raised corn, soybean, wheat and cattle.

William and Thelma.

Davee retired from full-time farming in 1986, but he continued to work with his son, Randy, who had taken over the farm, until 1999 when he suffered a stroke.

In his later years he enjoyed getting together for reunions with the men from his 233rd radar & searchlight battalion. Initially the reunions drew 50 or more people. Then it shrunk to just a dozen or more. Now, sadly, most of the men are gone or unable to travel.

In his final years, Davee lived with his son and daughter-in-law on the land he once farmed. From time to time he looked at the photos and mementos from his

One of the unit's reunions (Davee sitting on far right).

service days and remembered places and people from long ago and far away. But most of the time he was content to look at the land he once farmed and the people he had always loved — a family that had grown to include three grandchildren, two great-grandchildren and one great-great-grandchild.

William Davee died on December 25th, 2014 and was buried at Forest Lawn Memory Gardens in Greenwood, Indiana. He was 92.

William Davee, 2014.

KERMIT DAVIS
COMPANY I, 3RD BATTALION, 9TH REGIMENT, 3RD MARINE DIV.

NINTH MARINES

Duty on Two 'Jima' Islands
Marine Reflects on His World War II Service in the Pacific

"Jima" is a Japanese word that means island. The word is used in the names of some islands in the Pacific Ocean located within 600-700 miles south of Japan.

Most are familiar with the island of Iwo Jima — the site of one of the most horrific World War II battles between the Japanese and the Marines. It was also the location for the famous photo of Marines raising the U.S. flag on Mt. Suribachi.

But there is also another "Jima" island that is part of the Word War II drama. It is the island of Chichi Jima.

Marine Corps veteran Kermit Davis of Plainfield, Indiana became very familiar with both of those islands.

Born on November 16, 1925 in Vandalia, Ohio, Davis entered the Marine Corps in June of 1944. Initially, he decided on enlisting in the Navy because his brother was already serving as a sailor. But while he was standing in line to enlist in the Navy, a Marine took him out of that line and directed him to the line for enlisting in the Marine Corps. Davis walked back to the Navy line, and the Marine came back to him and redirected him again. "This time he stayed with me," said Davis. "He said, 'Marines are part of the Navy, too.'"

Following his six weeks of basic training at Parris Island, South Carolina, he completed BAR (Browning Automatic Rifle) school at Camp LeJeune, North

I Company, 3rd Btn, 9th Marines at Guam. Feb. 1945.

Carolina and then traveled across country to Camp Pendleton, California for some final training.

Assigned to Company I of the 3rd Battalion, 9th Regiment, 3rd Marine Division, he left with his unit in September of 1944 and headed for the island of Guam. His unit had been designated as combat replacements for the Allied effort that was already underway to take back the island of Guam from the Japanese who had invaded it shortly after the attack on Pearl Harbor.

By the time that Davis and the Marines of the 3rd Battalion arrived on Guam, the Japanese had been pushed into the interior of the island and were beginning to surrender. Some of them surrendered to Davis and the Marines of his unit.

Guam was also the site of his first confirmed kill. Thinking he was hearing the approach of the enemy, he called out for the password and, when there was no reply, he and some other Marines fired their weapon. The enemy turned out to be a water buffalo that had snuck up on the men. When the men were reprimanded by their unit officer, one of Davis' friends tried to defend the shooting by saying, "We called out for the password and the water buffalo didn't know it." Chuckling over the incident, Davis recalled that the U.S. government had to pay reparations to the local Chamorro natives for the unintended kill.

But combat was about to become much more dangerous for Davis.

After securing the island of Guam, the Marines began training for the next big island invasion. This one would take place on Iwo Jima, an 8 square mile island located 750 miles from mainland Japan.

Iwo Jima was considered to be prime real estate for Allied Forces, as its important airfield and proximity to Japan would allow U.S. fighter planes to escort heavy bombers on bombing missions to mainland Japan.

The battle for Iwo Jima began on February 19, 1945 and lasted for 36 days, officially ending on March 27, 1945. Some of the fiercest combat of the war occurred during those six weeks. At the end of the battle, over 19,000 Japanese lost their lives and close to 7,000 Marines were killed.

Battle at Iwo Jima.

Among those killed was Davis' company commander, who was shot in the head by a sniper. Davis also had to carry his wounded Lieutenant to safety after he became one of the 26,000 American casualties of the battle.

Davis, who served as a rifleman and company runner while on Iwo Jima, became a casualty as well when, on February 28th, he was wounded in the neck by the shrapnel from a Japanese hand grenade. He received a Purple Heart as a result of the injury and then spent the next 20 years digging out small parts of the grenade from his neck.

There were plenty of other times Davis could have been injured or killed. He recalled the time his battalion had been given the mission to take one of the island's hills in an area called Cushman's Pocket. Unbeknownst to them, they passed right through the enemy's line and took the wrong hill. "We were supposed to take hill 365, but we took hill 362 instead," Davis said. The error resulted in them being surrounded by the enemy. "It took another battalion about three days to come out and rescue us."

Although it was the wrong hill, his battalion received a Unit Citation for their bravery in holding out while surrounded by the enemy.

There were even some moments of humor in looking back at an otherwise awful time. On one occasion, cases of canned peaches that were stacked just outside of Davis' foxhole were blown apart by the shells of Japanese artil-

Remaining company at the end of 32 days of fighting, 1945, Iwo Jima. Kermit Davis, center back row.

Davis in March of 1945, after Iwo Jima battle.

lery. The cans contents were scattered over the men. "We didn't know what it was," remarked Davis. "At first, we thought we'd been splattered with flesh and blood from someone being hit. It turned out it was just the peaches and juice that showered us," chuckled Davis.

After securing Iwo Jima, the Marines of the 3rd Battalion returned to Guam where they began their training for the coming invasion of Japan. "I learned later that we were to invade Kyushu," Davis said.

It was an invasion that never happened. The Japanese surrendered on September 2, 1945 following the devastation of two atomic bombs dropped by the U.S. and the threat of the Russians who were set to invade Japan from the North

Not having enough points to be sent home, Davis was transferred to the 3rd Regiment in September of 1945 and then sent for occupation duty to another "Jima" island. This one was Chichi Jima.

Located 150 miles north of Iwo Jima, Chichi Jima is 15 square miles and located 600 miles south of Japan. The island was home to several long-range Japanese radio stations and was used as a key base of communication for the Japanese and the surrounding islands.

While not having the combat notoriety of its sister island to the south, Chichi Jima did have dark days for some of the downed U.S. Navy fighter and bomber pilots who were kept as prisoners on the island. Some of the pilots were severely beaten while others were executed. Further investigation after the war revealed that in some gruesome cases the executed pilots were even partially cannibalized by the Japanese military on the island.

Thirty enlisted Japanese soldiers were eventually convicted of war crimes by military court-martial. Four Japanese officers who were found guilty were put to death by hanging for their involvement in the crimes.

Davis and the other Marines sent to the island were tasked with receiving and processing the surrendering Japanese forces on the island (over 25,000 Japanese in the island chain surrendered after the war) and making sure there would be no resistance.

"We were sent to destroy all their fortifications and weapons," Davis said.

Davis recalled having time to visit with the Japanese translators/escorts that were assigned to them. "We would sit around and talk with each other," he said. "They would tell us about their experiences and how they wanted to go home. It was an interesting conversation."

An official surrender ceremony was held on Chichi Jima on December 13, 1945. During the ceremony each Marine received a Japanese officer's sword as a gift and peace offering.

Captured Japanese soldier on Chichi Jima.

Following his occupation duty on Chichi Jima, Davis returned to Guam and then boarded a ship to head back to the U.S. He was finally discharged in May of 1946, having attained the rank of a Corporal.

A few years later, Davis was back with the Marines on active duty. The Korean War had erupted and many of the World War II veterans were getting called back to active service. Davis was one of them.

In September of 1951, he found himself once again on an island. But this time he avoided the Pacific Ocean and landed instead in Puerto Rico, an island in the Caribbean. The college education he pursued after World War II allowed him to transfer from the Marine Infantry to the Marine Special Services and Recreation unit. He served as an Athletic and Recreation Assistant on Puerto Rico from September to November of 1951 and was discharged as a Sergeant in September of 1952.

Davis returned to the United States and married Jean Bailey in 1954. He had met her while working at a summer camp in Maine. The couple went on to raise two sons: Kyle and Kelly.

Davis graduated from the University of Dayton with a history degree and went on to earn his Master's degree at Xavier University in Ohio. He taught history and coached football in Troy and in Brookfield, Ohio before accepting a position at Plainfield High School in Indiana, where he taught and coached for 17 years. Davis retired from teaching and coaching in 1988.

Kermit Davis, teacher and coach, 2013.

Over the years Davis has reunited with his Marine Corps buddies at reunions in country and abroad. For many years, the Marines who served on Chichi Jima held reunions in Pennsylvania.

Davis has also returned to Iwo Jima for reunions on three different occasions. He visited not only with the men of his battalion but the former Japanese soldiers who fought there as well. On one trip he took his sons and grandson with him. During one visit he was interviewed by television personality Ed McMahon.

Each year in Nobelsville, Indiana there is also a Central Indiana reunion for Marines who served on Iwo Jima. The ranks of attendees have thinned considerably, but the men who are left still enjoy getting together.

Davis was on the inaugural Indy Honor Flight to Washington D.C. in September of 2012. He was honored again by his Plainfield community when he was selected to be the Grand Marshall for the annual Quaker Days Parade in Plainfield, Indiana, where Davis and his wife still reside.

An Unlikely Pilot Takes to the Sky
Cincinnati Native Flies P-47 in South Pacific

Some men grew up with aspirations of flying aircraft in support of World War II. But not Robert Donnelly of Indianapolis! "I didn't know the front of a plane from the rear," he admitted. But that didn't stop the recruiter in Cincinnati from slotting Donnelly for pilot training with the Army Air Forces.

The Cincinnati native was born on August 20, 1924. He enlisted in early 1943 after graduating from Elder High School. He knew that the draft was likely to catch him, so he decided to sign up on his own.

Donnelly completed his Basic Training in Miami Beach, Florida. "Worst place I was ever at," he recalled. He lived on the 7ᵗʰ floor of a hotel, and there were no elevators. "I never saw the beach until Glen Miller came for a concert toward the end of basic training," he said.

Following basic, he went off to Clemson University for College Training Detachment. The Army Air Force had so many pilot candidates in training that they had to send many of them for college training just to buy time to get them into the pilot training pipeline. Donnelly recalled, "Clemson University turned out to be one of the best places I was ever stationed." During his 6-8 weeks there he studied navigation, and took some other college subjects.

2nd Lt. Donnelly in the cockpit.

His pilot training regimen began in Montgomery, Alabama with Pre-Flight School. "I didn't know what I was doing at first," he said. "I just did what they told me to do." From Pre-Flight he went to the Basic Flight School in Augusta, Georgia. He then completed his Solo Flight Training in Camden, South Carolina. He finally earned his silver wings after completing Advance Flight Training in Marianna, Florida. Along with his wings came the rank of a 2nd Lieutenant.

Looking back over the 9 months of flight training Donnelly said, "I guess I enjoyed it; because I wound up as a pilot!" It was no small accomplishment. Many men washed out of flight training (up to 25% in 1943) if they couldn't master knowledge of the plane and demonstrate the skills needed for flying. At the conclusion of all of his flight schools, Donnelly was slotted to fly the P47 Thunderbolt (nicknamed "Jug"), which became the Army Air Force's best fighter-bomber. "I didn't like it at first", he said, noting its huge size (it was the biggest fighter at the time). "But I soon came to love it. It went on to earn the reputation for having the most kills in WWII," Donnelly said proudly.

Donnelly was assigned to the 1st Fighter Squadron of the 413th Group in the 301st Wing, which was headquartered in South Carolina.

After getting indoctrinated into the squadron, the new pilots headed out to Northern California. They were flown to Hawaii and received their personal planes somewhere in the Pacific. "I was thrilled to finally get it," Donnelly recalled of climbing into his new plane.

He named it "Cincy Belle," honoring his hometown roots. The name of his plane helped Donnelly meet the famous actor, Tyrone Power, who was a Marine Corps pilot. "I met him in Saipan in the PX," recalled Donnelly. "We were both from Cincinnati, so we had lunch together."

Originally, Donnelly's 1st Fighter Squadron was supposed to go to Okinawa to begin their combat flight duty. But they ended up on the island of Ie Shima instead, because the Army had not yet secured Okinawa for safe flight operations. "The Marines had to finish the job," Donnelly recalled.

Most of Donnelly's combat flight missions were over Kyushu, Japan, which was the most southwesterly of Japan's main islands as well as its third largest island.

P-47N Thunderbolt in flight.

Targets included factories, airfields, ships and radar stations. "We went to China also," said Donnelly. "We were closer to China than we were mainland Japan."

All of flights were hazardous combat missions. "The Jap Zeros were out there," Donnelly recalled. But they were not as dangerous as the Japanese artillery, which became a constant nemesis for Donnelley and the other pilots. All of the missions were frightening. "I said the Hail Mary a lot of times," said Donnelly.

Donnelly flew both strategic and tactical missions. Strategic missions included escorting B-29 Superfortress bombers in their bombing missions over Japan. Tactical missions were dive-bombing runs and napalm drops on Kyushu, Japan.

Fortunately for Donnelly, the P-47 was built to take a licking. And most of the time, enemy fire didn't penetrate the steel skin. "Jap 30 caliber rounds would bounce off the airplane," he recalled. "That airplane worked like a clock. It was built to take a beating. Maneuverability was out of sight! And we had good ground crew support."

Donnelly was in Okinawa when he heard of Japan's surrender. "I went up to Tokyo to participate in the fly by, which was scheduled to take place during the surrender ceremony," said Donnelly. "But MacArthur canceled it at the last minute. I guess he didn't want to scare the Japs more than what we had already done."

The trip to Tokyo wasn't a total waste of his time though. While there, he met and became acquainted with a Japanese combat pilot, who had been a Commander of a squadron of Jap Zeros. "He was a Harvard grad, and he spoke perfect English," said Donnelly. "He and I became very good friends for the week there."

It was a strange experience for Donnelly, who had spent over a year trying to destroy Japanese combatants. "One day I hated him, and the next day I loved him," said Donnelly, recalling the almost surreal reversal of attitudes.

Squadron pilots, with Donnelly standing, back row, second from left.

While in the Pacific theater, he also made it to China. "I've been to Shanghai in the air and on the ground," he said. "I preferred the ground as a tourist, but I'd rather be in the air during combat."

By war's end, he had completed a total of 38 combat missions, the last three from off the island of Okinawa. All total, he spent one and a half years in combat duty overseas.

Donnelly was decorated for his heroism in aerial combat, receiving the Distinguished Flying Cross from then Brigadier General Jimmy Doolittle on Ie Shima, Okinawa.

Donnelly returned to the U.S. in the fall of 1945 and was discharged from military service. He used the GI Bill to attend the University of Cincinnati, where he earned dual majors in English and Psychology. College was the first time he attended school with girls, as his prior schooling had been in an all-boys Catholic schools. He graduated in 1949.

Donnelly married Claire Kortecamp in 1949. They had lived in the same neighborhood while growing up. The couple raised two sons: Kevin and Keith. Their family grew to include 6 grandchildren and 4 great-grandchildren. "It was a good Catholic marriage," said Donnelly. It was also a long one, reaching 64 years together before Claire's death in November of 2013.

Donnelly in 2015, holding his service photo poster.

Donnelly's first job out of college was with Kroger in Cincinnati. He worked there for 10 years. In 1960 he moved his family to Indianapolis to work for Stokely Van Camp, where he was in charge of running the Gatorade program. He remained there until well into his 70s before he retired.

Donnelly returned to the air in May of 2014 to participate in the Indy Honor Flight trip to Washington D.C. "It was good," he said. "I had a real nice lady as a guardian to push me around in the wheel chair. They treated us like celebrities! It meant a lot to me. It gave me a shot in the arm for my patriotism. I even met Bob Dole. That was quite an experience! I talked to him for 5 minutes." The whole day brought Donnelly full circle from his days as a combat pilot. "I even met a guy on the plane to DC that I had been with in flight school."

His Silver Wings have long ago been placed under the protective glass of a picture frame. The one-time unlikely combat pilot has mostly good memories from his days of serving his country in the air. "I have a great feeling for America," he said. "I was proud to have been one of the millions in the service who made a contribution."

Donnelly died at the age of 90 on May 10, 2015. He was buried with military honors at Crown Hill Cemetery's field of Valor in Indianapolis.

P-47D Thunderbolt 318 fighter group with bazooka rocket tubes Miss Mary Lou Saipan 1944.

P-47 Thunderbolts from the 318th Fighter Group taking off from East Field on Saipan, Marianas Islands in October 1944.

Providing a Base For Fire

Soldier Carried 45-Pound Plate for Mortar Team

Teamwork is essential in military operations. That is especially evident with a mortar team. Each man must perform his function perfectly for the weapon to be fired.

Caryl Farrell understands well the concept of teamwork. The World War II veteran carried the essential base plate from which his team's 81-millimeter mortar gun was fired.

Born on Christmas Eve of 1924, Farrell grew up in Mattoon, Illinois. He attended several years of education at Mattoon high school before withdrawing.

Soldiers prepare an 81mm motar.

Farrell was drafted into the Army at the end of 1941, shortly after the attack on Pearl Harbor. He reported for basic training at Fort Walters in Weatherford, Texas. "We lived in tents there the whole time", he recalled.

Initially, Farrell was assigned to a rifle company. But later in his training he was tagged to become part of an 81 millimeter mortar team and was assigned the job of carrying the heavy base plate that the mortar tube fired from. "It was all right", said Farrell. "But it was heavy!" Forty-five pounds to be exact!

The mortar was a tubular weapon that fired projectiles from the ground. Developed in France and used some in World War I, it became an essential weapon during World War II. Referred to by some as "infantry artillery", the mortars were vital in the field of battle as they were easily transported and able to be quickly set up. They were used extensively in providing heavy fire power against the enemy.

A. Three-quarter front view of Model 97 81 mm infantry mortar showing shell next to baseplate. B. Close view of elevation mechanism.

Weighing about 136 pounds completely assembled, the mortar weapon consisted of a firing tube, a bi-pod, and a base plate, each weighing about 45 lbs. The four men assigned to a mortar team each carried a piece of the equipment and each man had a special job in readying the gun for fire. Farrell recalled having lots of practice setting up and firing the mortar gun during training.

At the end of basic training, Farrell was assigned to the Army's 27th Division and sent by train to California. From there he and the members of the division were transported to Oahu, Hawaii to defend the outer islands from any further attack by the Japanese.

While stationed on Oahu, Farrell stayed in Schofield Barracks, which wasn't far from Honolulu — a favorite spot for spending liberty. The training on Oahu lasted for several months as the Division prepared for combat operations in the Marianas Island chain.

By late spring, the Division was on its way across the Pacific Ocean for a rendezvous with the Marines off the coast of Saipan. The 27th Division made their amphibious landing on June 16th, 1944. "It was scary", recalled Farrell. "People were getting shot and we saw dead bodies on the beach." The Japanese had the high ground and were shooting down upon the advancing forces.

As if combat wasn't bad enough, Farrell also had to deal with the other island enemy — mosquitoes. "I developed malaria there", he said.

Combat operations on the island lasted until the end of June. "We set up our 81 mortar every time we went near the front lines", he recalled. "I don't remember how long we were there. I just did what they told me."

Even after the island had been secured, there was still mop up duty to perform. Throughout July and August of 1944, the division was used to clear out pockets of enemy forces still hiding out in Saipan's mountains.

In the middle of August the 27th Division was transported to New Hebrides Island for rest and replenishment. And by November, Farrell had enough points earned to return home to the States.

He traveled by ship back across the Pacific Ocean on a troop transport that included a group of Japanese POWs that were being taken to the U.S. for internment.

Discharged at Great Lakes Naval Base in Chicago, Farrell returned home just before Thanksgiving. "I was glad when it ended", he said. "If felt good to be back home." His homecoming in Mattoon included a ride in a convertible down Main Street.

Farrell got on with his life as a civilian. He worked for a while on the Illinois Central Rail as a fireman before coming to Indianapolis and driving for the Mayflower moving company.

Farrell with his
World War II Victory Medal.

While he was in Indianapolis, he met and married his first wife. When that marriage ended, he returned to Illinois and worked on a truck, spotting trailers for a company that made lawnmowers.

Employment opportunities then took him to Arizona, where he worked for a time in construction before getting a job as a driver with Dial a Ride in Tempe. He held that job until 2004. Farrell then became a monitor for a school bus in Mesa, Arizona, working until his retirement in 2012.

Farrell and his second wife, Marsha (he had remarried in 1991) moved to Martinsville in 2012 to be closer to his wife's daughter. Marsha died a short time later.

Adorning Farrell's wall are two things that commemorate important periods of his life. One object is a plaque that identifies him as "Monitor of the Year" in 2007-2008 for Mesa Public Schools. "It was one of my favorite jobs," he said. The other object is a picture frame that encases his World War II Victory Medal. Of that he says, "I am real glad I was able to help save the country."

American mortar team in action during fierce fighting around Ormoc, Leyte, in December, 1944.

Mortar team fires rounds during WWII in France.

Bomb Raids on Tokyo

Veteran Served as B-29 Radar Operator High Over the Pacific

George Gladden of Clayton, Indiana has spent most of his life close to the Indiana soil that he has tilled as a farmer. But for a couple of years during World War II he was as far away from the Hoosier soil as one could be — 6,457 miles west and about 32,000 feet above it, to be more precise!

Born George Lester Gladden on May 11, 1922 he was raised on a farm in Bridgeport, Indiana. After graduating from high school he worked at Allison Transmission in Speedway for two years before World War II interrupted his life, as it did for some 16 million other young men and women. Gladden referred to his draft notice as the "greeting (from Uncle Sam) sent to him."

Gladden was drafted into the Army Air Force at the age of 20 in December of 1942. Following basic training he went to a series schools: radio school in Sioux Falls, South Dakota; radar school in Boca Raton, Florida; gunnery school in Fort Myers, Florida; and flight training at Walker Air Base in Hayes, Kansas.

At the conclusion of his year and a half of training he was assigned to the 20th Air Force, 73rd Bomb Wing, 500th Bomb Group, 883rd Bomb Squadron. It was a squadron consisting of the most recent additions to the arsenal of aerial bombers; the massive B-29 Super Fortresses — the same planes that would eventually drop the atomic bombs on Hiroshima and Nagasaki. The plane he was assigned to was

167

George's B-29 ,"Fancy Detail."

named "Fancy Detail." The tail of the plane sported a painting of a young woman in a bathing suit.

Gladden was one of eleven crewmembers assigned to his plane.

As a radar operator he was positioned in the rear of the aircraft in a darkened pressurized compartment. And he was responsible for tracking enemy aircraft by peering through a rubber sleeve that enveloped a screen from the APQ-13 radar system. Gladden would see blips of light appear

1. Maj. James S. Braden, AC 2. 1st Lt. Eugene C. Petersburg, Pilot
3. 1st Lt. Oscar N. Korsmo, Nav 4. 2nd Lt. Donald G. Wilson, Bomb
5. 1st Lt. Sigmund J. Rusen, Flt/Eng
6. S/Sgt. Robert C. Cunningham, Lft Gunr 7. S/Sgt. Sammie M. Stulz, Tail Gunr
8. S/Sgt. Haakon F. Myrwang, Radio 9. S/Sgt. Zachary T. Everett, Ring Gunr
10. S/Sgt. George L. Gladden, Radar 11. Cpl. Charles Woodward, Rgt Gunr

Braden Crew   Z Square 50 Aircraft "Fancy Detail"

as planes — friendly or foe came into the area of his plane. Radar was used for bombing in overcast conditions as well as an aid to navigation and enemy plane detection.

His squadron left the U.S. in November of 1944 and reported for duty at the B-29 air base in Saipan, located in the Mariana Islands. "It took us 29 hours to fly to Saipan", he recalled of the trip, and then added, "and it took 29 DAYS to return to the U.S. (by ship)"!

The squadron's mission was to bomb Japan, specifically Tokyo. Gladden's plane departed for its first bombing raid on Tokyo on November 24, 1944. He recalled of that first mission, "We flew from Saipan to Japan which was 1,500 miles one way over water. And if you had any trouble there was no place to park it. You just had to ditch it."

Getting to the bomb location was only part of the danger to the B-29 crews. Avoiding being shot down while flying over the targets was the other danger.

Initially the bomb runs were flown at the safe altitude of 30,000 feet. Japanese fighters struggled at that altitude and few were able to keep up with the speed (up to 350 mph) of the B-29.

After discovering that a powerful jet stream from Siberia at 20,000 feet was blowing the bombs off target, orders came down for the B-29's to fly at the much lower altitudes of 8,000 feet … at night … and approaching the target one at a time instead of in groups. Not only were the B-29's more visible to anti-aircraft fire, they were also much more vulnerable to attack by Japanese fighter planes.

"When you get to Japan, the fighters would meet you and they would try to pick you off," Gladden said. "Once in a while they would get a few of us. And then you get over the target and they (fighter planes) backed off and they had the ground gunners take over. The flak would be so heavy out there you could pretty near walk on it. But we were lucky! We got a few little holes but nothing which knocked us out."

Many B-29s and their crews were lost even before ever making it up in the air. The planes were so big and loaded to maximum capacity with bombs that there was no cushion for failure in takeoffs. "Our biggest fear was takeoffs," Gladden recalled. "If you got two-thirds of the way down the runway and one of them engines coughed, you didn't have time to stop. You'd just end up in the ocean!"

When the Marine Corps invaded the island of Iwo Jima and secured her air fields in late March of 1945, the P-51 Mustangs were finally in a position to accompany the B-29s on their bombing runs, making it safer for Super Fortresses.

B-29 dropping firebombs, Yokohama, May 29, 1945.

Bomb loads changed from the heavy bombs to the incendiary bombs in March of 1945. Tokyo came under fire from hundreds of B-29's dropping 150-pound shells with the highly flammable, jelly-like substance. "As far as you can see, the whole town was on fire," Gladden recalled of the aftermath of those bombs.

On August 6th and 9th a B-29 dropped the most famous bomb load of all — the atomic bomb; which finally brought the empire of Japan to the surrender table.

Gladden was on his way back home on a transport ship when it was announced on the ship that the war had come to an end. He received his discharge on November 7, 1945 and left the service as a Staff Sergeant with 35 successful bombing missions, a Distinguished Flying Cross, and an Air Medal with Four Oak Leaf Clusters.

B-29 Superfortress bombers of US 73rd Bomb Wing flying near Mount Fuji, Japan, 1945.

Returning to his native Indiana after the war, Gladden went back to the soil he had missed and resumed work on a farm. But farming wasn't his only focus. A woman named Mary was on his mental radar.

Gladden had met Mary, who is originally from West Virginia, at an Arthur Murray dance club in Columbus, Ohio where he was stationed for a time during his military service. The two visited with each other several times before Gladden left for the war.

When he arrived in San Francisco on his return from combat in 1945, he called her on the phone and they arranged to meet at the train station in Chicago for a reunion visit. It wasn't until she arrived in Chicago that she realized she didn't know which station Gladden would be arriving at. By the time Gladden found her — she was at the wrong station— it was 4 a.m., and she was still waiting for him. Her devotion was rewarded when Gladden married her. Together they raised a family. They have been married for 64 years.

Today, at the age of 93, Gladden continues to farm about 80 acres in Clayton with his son.

He briefly returned to the skies in September of 2012 on the inaugural Indy Honor Flight — a trip to Washington D.C. to see the World War II Memorial.

Commenting on his time back on a plane again Gladden replied, "I kind of enjoyed it." He said to the pilot on the way off the plane, "That's about the smoothest airplane ride I ever took. It was a little bumpy on the landing." The pilot replied, "Yeah, I finally found the runway."

George Gladden is proud to have served his country high over the waters of the Pacific. And he is grateful to have found the safe runway back home after the war.

Gladden on the inaugural Indy Honor Flight, 2012.

Bomber of the 500th BG on their hardstands circa 21 Oct 1944, Saipan, Marianas Islands, 881st Squadron.

Treasures from War

Veteran's War Mementos Passed on to Daughter

Treasures are often found inside small chests; like the type used to keep prized jewelry or other items of sentimental value.

Virginia Holsapple of Martinsville, Indiana, has her own prized chest of treasures. It is the wooden box filled with mementoes of her father's service during World War II.

Carl W. Hawkins served in the U.S. Army with the 132nd Infantry in the Asiatic Pacific. He didn't just fight. He gathered and collected items from the far-away places that he served. And he gave those treasures to his daughter before his death in 2003.

Born on May 3, 1923 in Trafalgar, Indiana, Hawkins was the second of five children raised by his parents Joseph Hawkins and Viola Pearl Foster.

He attended Cook Hollow and Helensburgh Schools up through his freshman year.

On February 11, 1943, at the age of 19, he entered the Army at Fort Benjamin Harrison in Indianapolis. Brothers Emmanuel (Navy) and Joseph (Army) also joined the war effort.

Hawkins was trained as a combat infantryman and as a truck driver. By the end of October, 1943 he was on his way to combat in the Pacific theater of war.

U.S. Soldiers at Bougainville(Solomon Islands) March, 1944.

He recorded a few of his reflections while on ship in a small spiral notebook. Some were happy reflections. "The sun looked nice shining on the water." But other statements were more sobering. "I knew that each day out was that much farther from home."

And he wondered of the danger that lay ahead on the trip across the sea, and whether he was ready for it. "A guy never knows what is going to happen next. I wish I did know so that I could be ready for it."

Ready or not, he arrived on the island of Fiji in November of 1943 and was assigned to the 132nd Infantry Regiment, the Americal Division. The regiment was on rest and refit on the island of Fiji after participating in combat on Guadalcanal.

In January of 1944, the 132nd arrived on the island of Bouganville (in the South Solomon chain of islands) for operation Cherry Blossom. Their mission was to confront and push out the Japanese forces that had occupied the island since 1942.

During combat there Hawkins was injured on April 4, 1944. Holsapple recalled her father telling her that he was down in a foxhole and had just turned around to get his rifle when he was hit in the back of the head with shrapnel or a bullet fragment. He turned around and was then hit again by shrapnel, this time on the side of his mouth.

He was sent to a hospital in the Philippines and, following his recovery, returned to combat. But a nasty scar marred his upper lip. He grew a moustache to hide it. It was a moustache that he would wear for the rest of his life.

After pushing the Japanese out of Bouganville, the Army directed its attention to freeing the Philippine Islands. In late March of 1945, the 132nd Regiment made an amphibious landing on the island of Cebu and thereafter secured Opon Airfield and Mactaw Island before being inactivated in the late fall of 1945.

After two years and 28 days of service abroad, which included combat duty in the Northern Solomon Islands and the Philippines, Hawkins returned to the U.S. in November of 1945. The Purple Heart recipient received his honorable discharge and came back to Indiana.

Holsapple recalled hearing that her father was not in good health at his return. "When he came home he was in bad shape with jungle rot," she said. "The bottom of his feet were gone. He doctored on them for years."

As Hawkins was getting discharged from the Army at Camp Atterbury in Indiana, he met Ruth Esther Hacker from Morgantown, who was working there as a cook and nurse's aide. The couple dated for the next ten months, and were then married in October of 1946.

Carl and Ruth Wedding, Oct. 1946.

"We used to tease him that he was a cradle-robber," Holsapple said, referring to the seven year age spread between the 23 year old Hawkins and the 17 year old Hacker.

Their daughter, Virginia Jean, was born a short time later. She would be their only child, and she would grow up to admire and love her father.

Hawkins worked for a time painting water towers. Holsapple recalled her father taking her with him and placing her on a blanket as he climbed the tower he was painting.

Carl, Ruth and Virginia, 1948.

When time permitted, he sought the solace of hunting (coon and rabbit were his favorite targets) and fishing.

As Holsapple grew older, Hawkins started showing some of his war mementos to her. She grew to treasure the chest filled with his dog tags, medals and ribbons. And she found especially interesting the items he had gathered from far-away places: a Japanese flag, an oriental hair comb, a pipe, a necklace, a spoon and other 'jewels' from the Orient.

Carl and Virginia, 1948.

Carl in 1992 at age 70 in his VFW uniform.

Virginia, holding her father's Purple Heart medal.

She recalled showing some of her father's war mementos to her friends. "I used to bring kids over to the house to show them Dad's war stuff."

Hawkins worked as a mechanic for International Harvester in Indianapolis before buying into Standard Oil and operating a service station in Paragon for 30 years, retiring at the age of 60.

Hawkin's wife, Ruth died in 1981.

In retirement he moved down to Florida and enjoyed ten years in the warmth and sunshine. He was active in the VFW and the Disabled American Veterans.

Holsapple moved her father back to Martinsville in 1993 to be close to her after he suffered an aneurysm. A stroke later followed. "The local DAV was so good in helping with medicine and things when he came to live with me," Holsapple said.

Hawkins turned to dancing for his therapy. He had taken up the activity later in his life and it became the primary motivation to getting him back on his feet after his stroke.

After he came back home, Holsapple discovered that her father was afraid of the dark and terrified of unknown sources of light. When she asked him about his fear he replied, "Sis, if you saw what I saw in the war you would be scared too."

"I'll always leave a light on for you dad," she assured him. To this day, she keeps a solar light on his gravestone.

Holsapple also recalled her father's reaction to watching World War II movies on television. "When he watched television he'd say, 'If only people knew. That is nothing like what we went through! But I would do it again!'"

Even with his right arm crippled from the stroke, Hacker would salute the big American flag at Community Chrysler in Martinsville whenever he and his daughter would drive by. "He would use his good left hand to raise his paralyzed right to make a salute," Holsapple recalled. And then he would say, 'Sis, your dad helped put that flag up there.'"

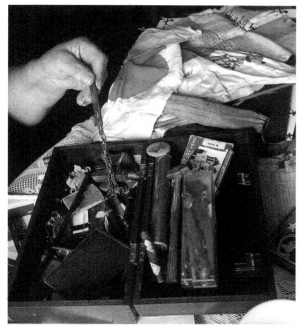

Chest of Carl Hawkins' military mementos.

"The flag is the most beautiful thing in the world to me", she said.

Holsapple recalled her father telling her, "Always remember, life is nothing but memories. So make them good."

She has nothing but good memories of her father. And a treasure chest of objects from a war he fought long ago. "I wouldn't trade this for the world", she said. "When I go through the box I wonder what went through his mind and where it came from."

Virginia holding her father's Japanese flag.

US Army troops from the Americal Division, 132nd Infantry Regiment take cover after their amphibious landing at Cebu. Credit: US Army. Date: March 26, 1945.

Cooking Through Combat
Hoosier Supports War Effort By Making Food

World War II was won with men, weapons and equipment. And it was also won with food! Armies don't win wars on empty stomachs. That's why there are Army cooks. And John Lofland was one of them.

Born on October 30, 1922, the oldest of five, the Montgomery County, Indiana resident graduated from Waynetown High School. Following the U.S. entrance into World War II he decided to enlist in the U.S. Army. He was assigned to the position of cook. He attended basic training at Camp Lee in Virginia and completed his training at Camp Ellis in Illinois.

Assigned to the 234th Salvage Collection Company in the fall of 1943, he departed from the U.S. on an English ship and headed to the South Pacific. The ship passed through the Panama Canal and took 30 days to cross the Pacific Ocean. They disembarked at Milne Bay, New Guinea. Lofland was selected as the cook for 17 officers and enlisted men and sent on an intelligence-gathering mission to Finschhafen, New Guinea for several months.

It was while he was in New Guinea that Lofland experienced one of the high points in his cooking service. The Seabees (Naval Construction Forces) were nearby cutting down some palm trees for road construction. Lofland had heard that a salad could be made out of the "heart of the palm." He arranged to extract the "hearts" from the cut palm trees and promptly treated his unit to fresh heart of palm salad. "They loved it", he said. "It was gone in no time!"

Example of an Army field range.

After a few months, the intelligence-finding group rejoined the rest of the company at Hollandia, New Guinea.

From New Guinea, the Salvage Collection Company was sent to Leyte, Philippines, landing there on October 26th, six days after the Allies invaded the Philippines to take it back from the Japanese. General MacArthur had waded ashore at Leyte two days earlier, on October 24th.

By this time, the Allied forces had taken control of the airfield, but the Japanese still harassed the Allies with frequent fly-over's and bombing.

For the next 12 months, the Salvage Collection Company did their work collecting items lost or discarded from battle; and Lofland did his work of keeping the 200 men unit fed. He used a special field mess oven that could be operated from a flatbed truck or on the ground.

When asked about his greatest challenge he replied: "Being able to make a palatable meal with the food available to you." It was difficult to get fresh food for the meals. Most of it came from cans. He was instructed not to use the food sold at the local market, as it might not be safe for consumption. Lofland kept his unit well fed and they finally completed their work.

While at Leyte, Lofland got a surprise visit from his brother, Luther, who was with the Army Air Forces just 30 miles from Lofland's location. Lofland later returned the visit by going down to see Luther when he was hospitalized.

Lofland was discharged from active duty in January of 1946, having honorably served for three years. He left the service and returned home to Indiana. He met his future wife, Lela, and they married on September 14, 1947. They raised four children: John, Carolyn, David and Natalie.

Though he was no longer needed on active duty following the end of World War II, Lofland decided to continue his service by joining the Army Reserve in Lafayette, Indiana. He served for eight years from 1946-1954.

Osaka Army Hospital.

In November of 1950, Lofland was mobilized for support in the Korean War. He attended some training in Fort Lewis, WA and then (for the second time in his life) headed across the Pacific. He made it as far as Japan, where he was assigned as cook at the Osaka Army Hospital. Here he learned "quantity cooking" — serving many more that the 200 men he cooked for during World War II. Fortunately, he had more and better cooking equipment at his disposal as well. "They even had steam tables to keep the food warm."

Lofland served in Japan through August of 1951. He eventually left the reserves in 1954, having amassed a total of four years active duty and eight years reserve duty service in the U.S. Army.

He returned home and continued with his career at Donnelley's, a printing business in Crawfordsville, Indiana. Before the war he had worked as a proofreader at Donnelley's. Upon his return from the service, Lofland became a linotype operator. He worked at Donnelley's for 47 years before retiring.

Lofland had one other recent highlight in connection with his former military service. On April 16, 2012 he was part of the inaugural trip of World War II veterans leaving from Lafayette, Indiana on an Honor Flight to Washington D.C. The trip was sponsored by the Greater Lafayette Gold Star Mothers Chapter. The Honor Flight Network is a national organization that provides free trips for World War II veterans to visit their memorial and other sites in Washington D.C. "It was an

Lofland and Filipino Men at WWII Memorial.

John Lofland, 2012.

emotional experience for me to be with other veterans and see the memorials." Lofland also enjoyed getting to know his guardian for the day, Ron Krause, a veteran of the Vietnam War. Guardians volunteer to assist the veterans they are assigned to as travel mates. And they pay their own cost for the trip. "We bonded as veterans and brothers and still keep in touch", said Lofland.

There was a special flashback moment for Lofland as he was standing at the World War II Memorial near the marker for South Pacific Islands. Two young Filipino men approached him and asked if he had served in the Philippines. When he said yes, they both shook his hand and expressed their appreciation for helping to free the country of their ancestry.

"What struck me," Lofland said, "was that neither these guys nor probably their parents were alive and living on the Philippines when I served there. It was their grandparents that were on the island with me. Two generations later — and no longer even living there — they still take the time to express gratitude for what we did to free them from Japanese occupation."

Another recent honor for Lofland was having the privilege of pinning 2nd Lieutenant bars on his grandson, who serves in the Air Force. "I was able to give him his first salute and receive a silver dollar from him," Lofland said, referring to the military tradition of a new officer presenting a silver dollar to the first enlisted person who renders him/her a salute.

At the age of 92, Lofland is still at home in the kitchen and regularly assists his wife, Lela with cooking. They live in Crawfordsville, Indiana.

War and Peace on a South Pacific Island
Veteran Remembers His Months on Ie Shima

Army Air Force veteran Tom MacPhee spent 8 long months on a South Pacific Island in 1945. While on that island he witnessed both the horror of war and the vision of peace.

Born Thomas B. MacPhee on June 11, 1921 in Nova Scotia, he was the younger of two sons raised by his parents, Howard and Eva May MacPhee.

The family moved to the U.S. when MacPhee was just two years old. His father had already begun work in Boston prior to the rest of the family's arrival.

"We spent the first night in jail near the border," MacPhee recalled, referring to that first day in which he and his mother and brother tried unsuccessfully to enter the United States. They were lacking the required border tax, so they had to spend the night in jail.

The family settled in Dorchester, Massachusetts (a suburb of Boston). But each summer the family would return to their native Nova Scotia to visit their grandparents and other relatives. MacPhee has warm memories of those childhood summers along the ocean.

In 1939, MacPhee graduated from Stetson High School in Randolph, Massachusetts.

Tom at Halifax Proving Ground, 1942.

Following his graduation MacPhee got a job as a range clerk working at the Halifax Proving Range in Halifax, Massachusetts. His primary job was testing the 20 mm ammunition for the British Admiralty Technical Mission. The ammunition had to pass certain requirements on high/low trajectory as well as detonation. The duds were weeded out. He enjoyed the work and felt good about making a contribution to the Allied war effort.

On June 12, 1942, MacPhee married his high school sweetheart, Barbara Hill. Their marriage would be blessed with four children: Thomas, Marsha, Diane and Glen.

Six months after his wedding, on January 5, 1943, MacPhee, who had earlier received his draft notice, entered the U.S. Army Air Force. At the time, he wasn't thrilled with being drafted. "I felt I was doing far more for the war effort at home," he said, referring to his job of approving the 20 mm ammunition that would be used in the war.

**Tom with wife, Barbara, and son, Thomas —
July 1944.**

Following his basic training in Fort Devins, Massachusetts, he went to Fort MacDill in Florida for technical training in photographic intelligence.

While receiving additional training in Nebraska, MacPhee, who had begun the process many months earlier, finally became a U.S. citizen. He stood before a Federal Judge in Lincoln, Nebraska and swore his allegiance to the country he had been living in for most of his life.

By spring of 1945, MacPhee departed from Spokane, Washington, and headed to the South Pacific for duty with the 507th Fighter Group. He spent 43 days in transit on a troop transport. "My bunk was 8 high," he recalled! "And there were still more above me."

Because of his civilian experience with testing the 20 mm ammunition, he was assigned to the 20 mm gun crew while underway. That suited him just fine. "I wanted to be topside in case we got hit," he said.

The ship traced the longer but more scenic route on their course, coming around New Guinea and past the island of Okinawa, before arriving at the island of Ie Shima (today called Iejima), which is located northwest of the island of Okinawa. The date of arrival was April 19, 1945 — one day after journalist Ernie Pyle was tragically killed by a Japanese machine

gunner on the same island. "We passed by a sign that the infantry had put up that read, 'We've Lost a Buddy Today,'" recalled MacPhee. It was a sober reminder of the danger that lay ahead.

MacPhee and the others who had just arrived on the island didn't have much time to reflect on Pyle's death. They were under fire themselves. "The first thing we did was to dig a trench," said MacPhee. "We got bombed every night by the Japanese. It was frightening!"

Toward the end of that first month, the fighting came under control as the U.S. forces established air superiority over the island.

MacPhee kept busy working in aerial photographic intelligence. On one occasion he was instrumental in stopping a bomber from dropping napalm on a POW camp containing American forces. "I had gone through the intelligence books and discovered a POW camp there," recalled MacPhee. "I rushed over to the pilot briefing room to inform them of the POW location. It was the most important effort on my part."

During some down time, MacPhee and others were tasked with building a new mess hall. "It was so nice that the officers took it over," MacPhee said, with sarcasm.

MacPhee saw the carnage of war on the island of Ie Shima. But he also got a close-up look at future peace. In late August of 1945, a peace delegation from Japan arrived on Ie Shima in a Betty Bomber with a big red cross (identifying the passengers as peace emissaries). They had come to sign the preliminary surrender documents prior to boarding a U.S. C-54 transport and heading to the Philippine Islands to meet with General MacArthur. MacPhee saw the Japanese delegation arrive on the island. And he also witnessed their departure for the Philippines as they were accompanied by Allied leaders.

Betty Bomber, Japanese envoy at Ie Shima.

The formal surrender ceremony took place a week or so later in Tokyo Bay on September 2, 1945 on the battleship U.S.S. Missouri.

MacPhee did not return home right away following the surrender of the Japanese. "When the war ended we were stuck there," he recalled. "I had the points to come home, but there was no way home at the time." It would be another four months on the island before MacPhee started his trip home. He left Okinawa on Christmas Day in 1945. "It was the best Christmas present I ever got!" he said.

It was a slow ride home with an unexpected stop in Pearl Harbor for some repairs to the ship. But he finally made it stateside.

Following his discharge on January 20, 1946, he returned home to Massachusetts and got a job as a cashier in the Bank Trust Company in Brockton. He climbed the ranks and eventually became vice-president.

He then worked for Remington Rand Recording and Statistical Company. He and his family moved to Speedway, Indiana when an office was opened in Indianapolis. For 20 years, MacPhee managed a staff of 75 ladies who processed information from little punched cards that held the medical history data of thousands of individuals.

MacPhee briefly returned to Boston in a work transfer. He finally retired from the business in 1989.

After his retirement he and his wife moved out to rural Martinsville, Indiana, and lived in a home that he and his son, Glen, built together.

His wife, Barbara, died in 2006, but MacPhee still reflects upon the memories of their 64 years together.

For many of those years they spent their summers in a peaceful,

Barb, a friend and Tom in Nova Scotia in 1988.

coastal cottage in Nova Scotia that MacPhee had purchased shortly after the war. "I was the first one to have a bath tub out there," MacPhee recalled. "They laughed at me at first. And then they all got one." He then added, "We loved it out there!"

MacPhee's thoughts return periodically to that island where warfare once raged and where comrades died. However, his thoughts most often are filled with gratitude for the peace that finally came, not only to that island so long ago, but to much of the world, including his home nation.

"It's a life I have thoroughly enjoyed and still do," he said. "It's the life my dad always wanted."

MacPhee holds a 20mm round.

187

507th Fighter Squadron P-47D Thunderbolt 42-27234 parked at Fritzlar Airfield (Y-86), Germany, April 1945.

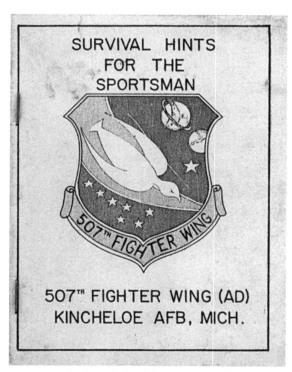

Survival guide booklet given to pilots.

Family Man on the Pacific
Hoosier Veteran Served on a Landing Ship

Most of the men who entered World War II were young, barely out of high school and without wives or children. But not David Martin! The Stinesville, Indiana native was a mature adult of 26 with a wife and children and a secure job when he entered the Naval Service in 1944.

Martin, who was born on April 11, 1918, was the youngest of seven children being raised by his parents Dean and Mattie Martin. He attended Stinesville High School through his sophomore year before entering the work force.

He married Dora Lavender on May 25, 1937. The two had met while Martin was eating at a restaurant where she worked. Before long, the newly married couple began building a family. Soon they were raising two sons: William Dewayne and Jackie Dewight.

Martin was a heavy equipment operator. He found work at the Maxon Construction Company in Dayton, Ohio and settled into establishing himself in a career and providing for his family.

In March of 1944, however, his life changed significantly when he left behind his wife, sons and job and was inducted into service with the U.S. Navy.

After completing his basic training at Great Lakes Naval Training Center outside of Chicago, Illinois, he departed for further schooling on the Virginia coast. He attended Basic Engineer Training in Norfolk, Virginia, and then finished up with Diesel Engineer Training in Little Creek, Virginia.

LSM 166 at anchor, location unknown.

Thereafter, he found himself assigned as a Machinist Mate to LSM 166 — one of the amphibious assault ships in the Landing Ship Medium class. The ship was brand new, having been commissioned in August of 1944. She was one of 558 LSMs built, most of which were assigned duty to the Asiatic-Pacific Theater of War.

The ship was 204 feet long and 35 feet in width. Her crew consisted of five officers and 54 enlisted men. She had cargo room to carry five medium tanks or 6 Landing Vehicles tracked along with accommodations for 48 additional troops.

Shortly after boarding his new ship, Martin was on his way across the Pacific Ocean and headed toward combat. As a Motor Machinist's Mate, Martin spent most of his time in the noisy and hot engine room.

From April 1 to June 30, 1945, LSM 166 was engaged in the assault and occupation of Okinawa Gunto, for which she earned one battle star.

LSM 166 off Okinawa.

Okinawa, 1945.

During the invasion, the enemy periodically fired upon her and she returned fire with her 40 mm and 20 mm guns as well. Martin wondered if he was going to make it home alive.

During one combat occasion there was an LSM in front of Martin's ship unloading high-octane fuel when a Jap Zero dropped a bomb. "It blew her up to bits," recalled Martin solemnly! "The only ones who survived were the ones who jumped overboard before the bomb's impact."

In September of 1945 the war came to an end with Japan's surrender. "After it was all done I was proud of serving," he remembered.

While there was much joy over the war's end, there was also much sadness over those who were killed in action. "I lost a lot of buddies," recalled Martin. "Some on the ship, some off the ship. It was a bad deal ... a bad deal!"

Martin returned stateside and was discharged from Naval service in November of 1945.

He reunited with his family and moved to Bloomington, Indiana. He and Dora added two more children to their family: Basil Dale and Dana Sue.

Martin worked for many years as a refrigeration and air conditioner mechanic for Price Electric and Indiana University. His final job was as a maintenance foreman at Bloomington Hospital in Bloomington, Indiana.

Later in life Martin built a house near Lake Lemon and enjoyed many years driving his 26 foot pontoon and fishing. His triumphs with the pole include a giant catfish that took four hooks before he was finally able to bring it in.

Martin held several memberships in community organizations including the Free and Accepted Masons, Lodge #74, Martinsville and The American Legion Post #18, Bloomington, Indiana.

He attempted to reach out to a few fellow sailors later in his life. "I wrote to two of them," he said, "but I never got anything back."

Martin's wife, Dora, died in 1990. Two of his four children have also passed on.

During his final years, Martin proudly wore his Navy ball cap and displayed his Certificate of Appreciation marking the occasion of the dedication of the World War II monument in Washington D.C.

Memories of 20 months of military service were never far from his mind — even while sleeping. "You wake up some nights and you are ready to shoot the guns," he said in reference to periodic flashbacks.

But overall, his life was one of peace and one of blessing. How else can anyone interpret the gift of a family that has grown to include 11 grandchildren and 19 great-grandchildren?

David Martin died on June 30, 2014 at the age of 96 with his loving family at his side. He was buried at Friendship Park in Paragon, Indiana.

NOTE: LSM 166 was decommissioned on May 2, 1946, at New Orleans, Louisiana. She was sold in October of 1947 to a company in New Orleans and converted to a barge.

Spared Again and Again
Veteran Recalls His Service in World War II

Ken Paschall is a grateful veteran of World War II. By his count, his life was spared six times from the grave dangers of war.

Born on June 24, 1925 in Independence, Missouri, Paschall was the oldest of three children. At the age of 15, and while still attending high school, he began working as a clerk at the Quartermaster Depot in Kansas City. "I worked a 6 hour shift (4–10 pm), 6 days a week, while attending high school," Paschall said. He remained at the job for three years.

Following his graduation in 1943, Paschall was drafted. He had been told before leaving the Army Quartermaster Depot that the Commanding Officer, a full Colonel, would write a letter of recommendation that he be sent to officer's training as soon as he completed his basic training. He was then to report back to the Quartermaster Depot and serve his active duty time there. It didn't quite work out that way.

When he arrived at the enlisted staging center in Leavenworth, Kansas, he was told by a non-commissioned officer that he would be entering the Navy. Still hoping for his promised commission in the Army, Paschall protested that he was vulnerable to extreme seasickness. He was directed to take a seat on a bench and somebody would get with him.

That "somebody" turned out to be a Marine. In Paschall's words, "After a while, a Marine Corps Master Sergeant came up to me, and the next thing I knew I was on board a ship as a Marine and I was headed to the South Pacific!"

869th Platoon, 1943.

Paschall first completed his basic training at the Marine Corps Recruit Depot in San Diego, California.

Following his basic training, he was to be sent to Guadalcanal to augment the combat forces there. But, just before his departure, his orders were suddenly changed, sparing him from the carnage of fighting on the island. He was directed instead for assignment to the 5th Anti-Aircraft Artillery Battalion, which came under the 1st Marine Division.

The battalion was sent to Kauai in the Hawaiian Islands, where they spent the next 18 months training on the new big guns (155 mm) the Marine Corps was testing in preparation for the upcoming battle on the island of Okinawa. "What a contrast!" said Paschall. Hawaii certainly beat out Guadalcanal for comfort and safety. That was his first experience with being spared.

He was not, however, spared from seasickness. Paschall's protest of entering the Navy due to seasickness turned out to be no empty threat. He recalled of his trip from San Diego to Hawaii, "I was deathly sick and ate very little for eight days out of the nine-day trip."

In late 1945, Paschall and his battalion boarded a ship and headed for the Ulithi Islands, which was to be the rendezvous point for the invasion of Okinawa. Upon reaching the island, he was in the third wave of the invasion forces. The

Tracers fired by the 5th Antiaircraft Artillery Battalion light up the night skies over Okinawa during a Japanese air attack. A Marine fighter squadron's Corsairs are in silhouette.

(DOD PHOTO (USMC) 08087 BY TSGT. C.V. CORKRAN)

invasion of Okinawa involved over 450,000 troops and 1,200 transports. Paschall's group settled in Kadena, on the southern part of the island, where they set up their antiaircraft guns.

For the next six months, Paschall would not be spared from combat, but he would be spared from serious injury ... barely!

Paschall recalled one close call with a Japanese plane that was firing upon their berthing area one night. "We were sleeping in tents when a group of Japanese 'Betty Bombers' dropped a bunch of bombs right over our tents. Be-

Artillery on Okinawa.

Tent Camp, Okinawa.

fore we got out, the shrapnel came through our tent from my side. All of it miraculously went right over my head. When we got outside after the bombing, we found a dead horse lying against the tent right on the other side of where I slept. He had taken all of the shrapnel that I would have gotten had he not been standing there."

Having been spared from harm, Paschall recalled an incident where he spared others. While on guard duty, some Japanese soldiers from the southern part of the island were trying to get to the north side to catch a transport back to Japan. Paschall caught them. He recalled, "I had orders to shoot, but since they weren't armed, I spared them."

Once the island of Okinawa was brought under Allied control, attention shifted to training for the planned invasion of mainland Japan. Paschall's 1st Marine Division was scheduled to be the spearhead division to enter Japan. Military planners projected that the invasion would be a bloodbath, as the Japanese would fight ferociously to protect their homeland and die for their emperor.

But, once again, Paschall (as well as many thousands of other Marines and soldiers) was spared from the onslaught, thanks to President Truman's decision to drop the atomic bomb over Japan. Paschall remembered, "We were watching a movie at our outside theater when the chaplain got up on the stage and told us that Japs had surrendered. The guys went nuts!"

The end of the war did not bring Paschall home right away. "I was hoping to go home," he said. "But I didn't have enough points. So, I was put into a group of Marines that was sent to Tientsin, China to repatriate the Japs and Germans back to their homelands."

Paschall served in North China for six months. He operated a warehouse of supplies and had a platoon of Japanese soldiers as-

1st Marines enter Tientsin.

Ken (standing far right) with other Marines.

signed to him for assistance. While there, he earned his promotion to Sergeant, just before being sent home in the spring of 1946.

After his honorable discharge, Paschall reported back to work at the Army Quartermaster Depot in Kansas City, where he served for the next three years as a senior draftsman and worked with the Army Corps of Engineers.

Paschall married his wife, Eileen, in April of 1950, just weeks before he was called back to active duty service in 1950 in support of the Korean Conflict. "I didn't even know I was in the reserves," Paschall said with surprise.

He returned to California for training. He was boarding a ship for combat in Korea when he suddenly was spared once again from potential harm. President Truman had issued an order stating that if a man had served in combat during World War II, he did not have to go to Korea for combat unless he wanted to volunteer. "I didn't want to volunteer," said Paschall. "So, they sent me to San Diego

Paschall with Eileen and their three sons, Steve, Kevin and Tom.

to serve as a drill instructor at the Marine Corps base for a year."

"I didn't mind it," Paschall said of his drill instructor duty, "but I didn't like it either. I tried to be rough, but I wasn't very good at it. But it was better than going to South Korea." After his year of service as a recruiter, Paschall was discharged again in January of 1951.

Paschall was almost again sent to Korea after finishing his year as a recruiter. A senior draftsman, signal corpsman was needed in Korea and Paschall was the only one in the division with that classification. His Colonel intervened and saved him from the deployment. "We did a lot of praying for two weeks," Paschall recalled of their waiting for the news that he wouldn't have to go.

After returning from California, Paschall attended the University of Nebraska and earned an Industrial Management Degree. He and Eileen got on with their lives and raised three sons: Steve, Kevin and Tom.

Paschall was hired at General Motors in Indianapolis, Indiana and worked there from 1954 to 1987 until he retired. His work involved finishing transmission castings for boats. He served as a foreman/supervisor as well as a plant manager.

In 2011, Paschall had a close call with death. He had a heart attack while walking on a darkened parking ramp. As he fell, he hit a concrete wall and sustained a concussion. But the impact jolted his heart back into rhythm enough so that he remained conscious to call for help. He was rushed to the hospital and during the next week almost died two additional times. Doctors inserted a pacemaker and Paschall has been good ever since.

Paschall's wife, Eileen, died in 2012. The couple had enjoyed 62 years of married life together.

Ken Paschall holding a shadow box dedicated to his military career.

Paschall has been actively involved in his Brownsburg, Indiana community. He has been an active member of his church and has spent significant time in civic activities. He even received a plaque from GM for outstanding community service.

The 89-year-old veteran remains active today. He still enjoys playing golf. "I play golf in the 80s every week," he said, "with a little help from the ladies tee."

And he still feels deep gratitude to God for the many times his life has been spared over the course of his nine decades.

Two Marines from the 2nd Battalion, 1st Marine Regiment during fighting at Wana Ridge during the Battle of Okinawa, May 1945.

BOB PATTERSON
COOK, *USS PROTON (LST 1078)*

Meaningful Words in War and in Life
Veteran Receives, Records and Shares the Gift of Words

Bob Patterson knows all about the importance of words. The Mooresville, Indiana veteran relied upon printed words from others to help get him through the war. After the war, he used words to instruct his students. And more recently he has used words to publish his life story and bless his family.

Patterson was born May 27, 1925 in Linnsburg, Indiana — a small town 10 miles southeast of Crawfordsville. When he graduated from Waveland High School in 1943 the U.S. was in the middle of World War II.

Because he worked as a farmer, Patterson had a deferment from military service. Like manufacturing, farming was deemed to be one of the essential careers for helping fuel the war effort. But it bothered him to stay behind as others went to war and performed their duty for country. So, a year after graduating, Patterson decided to enlist in the Navy.

On the day he turned in his deferment at the County Draft Office someone said to him, "Are you crazy?"

Patterson never regretted his decision. "It was one of the wisest decisions I ever made in my life," he said. "I doubt I would have ever gone to college if not for World War II." The GI bill encouraged 7.8 million of the 16 million who served in World War II to attend college.

LST-1078 putting troops and tractors ashore, Māʻalaea Bay.

Patterson left for boot camp in October of 1944. And, instinctively knowing that this would prove to be a life-changing adventure, he started recording his experiences in a diary — the same diary that he would use years later to write his book.

Following his training and schools Patterson was assigned as a cook on the *USS Proton* — a Landing Ship Tank (LST 1078) that carried troops and equipment. The ships were designed with flat bottoms that allowed them to get close to shore for amphibious landings.

After her shakedown cruise (the ship was brand new) in the Chesapeake Bay, she departed New York City in June of 1945 and headed to Pearl Harbor, HI via the Panama Canal. By the end of August the ship left Pearl Harbor on orders to take Army troops for occupation duty in Japan.

Although the war in the Pacific had officially ended with Japan's surrender on September 2nd, the danger to service members persisted. There were still mines in the ocean that threatened ship movement. And, this early in the surrender, no one knew for sure if Japan might not decide to re-engage in battle.

Furthermore, there was always the danger of crossing a foreboding ocean, especially on a LST. As Patterson explained, "The LST was flat-bottomed and terribly slow since it battered its way through the seas instead of slicing through the waves like a destroyer or cruiser. Little wonder that someone tagged it with 'Large Slow Target.'"

In addition to the trip to Japan, Patterson rode the slap-happy ship to the Philippines and the islands of Guam, Saipan and Tinian before finally making it back to Pearl Harbor.

It was during these long transits across the Pacific that Patterson turned to the printed words of others to comfort him in his loneliness and uncertainty about the future.

Prior to his departure for the Navy his parents had given him a steel-backed King James Bible. Inside those steel covers Patterson had placed a letter from his sister, Wanda. "She told me I was going to places where she and others who loved me could not go," recalled Patterson, "but there was One who loved me and would accompany me no matter what the circumstances happened to be. And that One was God!"

He read those words often during the next two years of service and drew peace and strength from them. Years later, he passed those words on to the next two generations of Patterson warriors. He gave the Bible and letter to his son, Greg who took them to the Mediterranean Sea when he served with the Marines on board an aircraft carrier. Today the Bible and letter are in the possession of Patterson's grandson, Drew, who serves in the Army. He took them with him on his combat tours to Iraq and Afghanistan.

Bob presenting the Bible that helped him so much to his grandson, Drew.

Patterson recalled a humorous incident of his time aboard *USS Proton* involved the ship's baker calling him into the kitchen one night. He showed Patterson that weevils had gotten into the bread dough. The supply officer's response to the situation was, "What's the vitamin content in those weevils?" Patterson recalls the officer telling the baker to roll away and make the bread.

"There were little black specks in the bread," recalled Patterson. "But no one but us ever knew what they were."

Patterson Family, 1963.

Another ancedote he recalled happened during his trip home from the war on a Landing Craft, Infantry (LCI 992). He said he received the best compliments for his cooking on that ship. One evening following dinner the commanding officer told him, "That was the best meal we've had in months!" Patterson recalled being a "one man show," working in his cooking space, which he referred to as a "cubicle with a grill."

After his discharge in October of 1946, Patterson returned home to Indiana. He met his future wife, Beulah the very first day after returning home from the war. He and his mother had gone to Producer's Dairy Creamery. In the front section there was a soda bar that served milkshakes. Beulah was the soda jerk who served Patterson and his mother.

"I took my mom home as fast as I could," Patterson recalled. He returned to the creamery and began his courtship. Patterson married Beulah a few years later on

September 11, 1949. He and Beulah started a family and enjoyed raising their three sons: Greg, Kent and Brad.

Patterson pursued a teaching degree at Indiana State Teachers College. Following his graduation he began a career in teaching, starting at the 6th grade and moving on to junior high. In 1965, Patterson accepted a position as the Assistant Superintendent at the Mooresville School Corporation, which he held until his retirement in 1985.

More recently in his retirement, Patterson has returned to the printed word to summarize his life story. And he has given those words as a gift to his family. His book, *Bob's Story,* was published by Author House in 2012.

Patterson was surprised a year or so ago to be the recipient of another special letter. While returning from the Indy Honor Flight trip to Washington D.C., he was handed a letter written by his grandson, Drew, who was serving in Afghanistan at the time. Drew filled three pages thanking his grandfather for his service to the country and for his love to their family.

Words of blessing have brought Patterson full circle in life. And they continue to enrich him today.

Patterson just before leaving on his Indy Honor Flight Trip.

LST ships, delivering men and equipment to Normandy Beach. Note the barrage balloons tethered to each ship; they were meant to deter dive-bombers and other low-flying aircraft.

A Bullet to Remind Him

Indiana Marine Survived Injury during Iwo Jima Carnage

Some veterans carry a visible mark on their bodies reminding them of their time of service in World War II. It might be a scar or a burn or even a lost limb. For Wayne Saucerman, it is a bullet fired from a Japanese rifle — a bullet that still remains in his leg — that serves as his reminder of war.

Saucerman, a Sullivan County, Indiana native born on May 1, 1926, was the third of six children born to his parents, Ray and Eva Saucerman. His older brother, Dean had served with the 1st Marine Division at Cape Gloucester. Deciding to follow his brother's example, Saucerman enlisted in the Marine Corps. He recalled, "I graduated (Sullivan High School) on Friday night (April 22nd, 1944) and was in the Marine Corps two days later (April 24th)."

He completed his 13 weeks of basic training at the Marine Corps Recruit Depot in Parris Island, SC and then moved up the coast to Camp LeJeune, NC for an additional two months of advanced infantry and combat training. He received training on the Browning automatic rifle, learned about demolitions and practiced amphibious landings on the beach.

Following his advanced infantry training, and after a five-day train ride across the country, he found himself in San Diego, from where he shipped off for Hawaii.

Saucerman recalled, "I got seasick while training in the Atlantic Ocean, so I thought I wouldn't get sick heading out from California. Before I got out of sight of land, I was sea sick!"

Dean and Wayne Saucerman.

Camp Maui, Hawaii served as a replenishment station for Marine units of the 4th Marine Division. The newly trained replacement troops were taken to the outdoor base theater to be assigned to infantry companies looking for replacements. The 4th Marine Division had recently returned to Hawaii from combat action at Saipan and Tinian and was in need of fresh troops as they prepared for what would be their most challenging battle yet — Iwo Jima.

While at the base theater on Thanksgiving Day, Saucerman was approached by a Marine Officer recruiting for replacements in a special scout and sniper platoon with the 24th Regiment. "Would you like to volunteer for this scout platoon," the officer asked Saucerman? Remembering that he was taught during training not to volunteer for anything, Saucerman didn't reply. "Well, I guess you are afraid of it then," the officer said in a loud voice, trying to embarrass Saucerman.

"No sir," Saucerman replied, "I'm not afraid of it, because I don't know what it is."

"So, you'll volunteer for it then?" the officer snapped back.

"Yes sir," replied Saucerman. And, from that moment on, he was part of an elite scout and sniper team with the 24th Regiment, 4th Marine Division.

He missed his Thanksgiving meal while getting processed into his new unit.

The platoon he was assigned to was made up of 33 and consisted of five-man squads. Each squad member carried a different weapon. Saucerman was assigned the BAR and also carried his M-1 rifle.

Saucerman and the Division remained at Camp Maui for a month, training with live fire as they prepared for actual combat.

On January 1st, 1945 the 4th Marine Division left Hawaii and began the journey across the Pacific for a rendezvous at Iwo Jima — a battle that was destined to become one of the iconic reminders of the war's carnage as almost 7,000 Marines died in the battle and over 19,000 were injured.

"We didn't know we were going to Iwo Jima until we left Saipan," Saucerman recalled, "and we didn't know a thing about Iwo Jima," he added. They were to learn all too soon of its horrors.

Group photo on Iwo Jima. Wayne is at the far right, bottom of the photo.

On February 19th, 1945 the Marines of the 1st, 4th and 5th divisions began their amphibious landing along the shores of Iwo Jima. Saucerman's platoon, scheduled to land at Blue Beach, didn't get to shore until later in the day. "I recall being in the rendezvous area for about four hours," he said.

At first the Marines in his LCP couldn't even see the island because of all the smoke the enveloped it from the bombs that were raining down from the Battleships. As his platoon got closer they could see the combat activity. In fact, some of that 'activity' came their way. As Saucerman explained, "Water splashed up as (enemy) mortars were landing on either side of our LCP (Landing Craft Personnel)."

When his group made landfall, they ascended three terraces under lots of small arm fire. They did the best they could to set up a defensive perimeter as the Japanese kept firing at them. The soft sand provided little assistance as the Marines tried to dig foxholes with their helmets, only to have most of the sand cave into the hole they had just dug. "The first night was touch and go!" Saucerman remembered of their efforts to survive through the first day.

The firing came from both in front and behind the Marines on the beach. The big artillery guns were firing close at hand from behind the men. "It was frightening," said Saucerman.

Stretcher bearers on Iwo.

The fear of enemy fire came also from the sky as Jap planes (referred to as "washing machine Charlie") flew over from Chichi Jima a few nights and dropped bombs on the men. One of the bombs landed next to the foxhole that Sacuerman was in. Fortunately, it was a dud! After the detonator was removed, the bomb squad, Saucerman had to carry the carcass of the bomb to the collection site to be sunk.

A few days after landing, Saucerman's platoon of 30 was called up to the front line for combat duty. "Only ten of us made it back (to the perimeter) after that operation," Saucerman recalled. Soon the ten would be reduced to five.

There were plenty of other close calls for Saucerman. His foxhole buddy, McCarthy, got hit while coming back to the hole one evening. On another occasion, Saucerman recalled finding a Japanese soldier inside a hole. Saucerman thought the man was dead, but when he went into the hole and picked up the man's leg, he discovered the enemy soldier was still very much alive. The Jap tried to detonate a grenade to kill both of them, but Saucerman was able to dispose of him.

February 23rd was the date of the historic flag-raising on the top of Mt. Suribachi. Although Saucerman's group was much farther down the shoreline, they were able to clearly see the stars and stripes flapping proudly in the wind. It was a great moment, but there was still more combat action ahead of them!

Saucerman recalled that every Marine on the island served as a stretcher-bearer at different times. It was hazardous duty to collect the dead as the firing from the Japanese continued. "There wasn't a safe place anywhere on the beach," said Saucerman. The dead Marines were buried in a trench, 36 inches from chest to chest and 6 feet deep, with a poncho covering each of them.

On March 15th, almost one month after their landing and just eleven days before the island was officially secured, Saucerman and several Marines from his platoon were involved in a cat and mouse operation of finding and firing upon the Japanese who were shooting weapons from the concealment of caves dug into the cliffs. Saucerman had been instructed to climb up on a ridge to help spot the enemy and direct the platoon's return fire at them. He did so, but a Japanese rifleman finally located his position and emptied three bullets into his body. One bullet hit him in the right hand and two in the right leg, leaving him with a compound fracture. Saucerman's war was over, but his battle for healing had just begun.

He was taken to the aid station on a stretcher. He waited 24 hours before he could get the medical attention he needed because so many other wounded Marines were ahead of him and had life-threatening injuries.

When he came out of surgery, he discovered that the surgeons had treated his hand wound, removed a bullet from his leg, inserted a rod into his broken femur to keep it stable and wrapped him from chest to right foot in a body cast. For some reason, perhaps because it wasn't deemed to be a health threat, the doctors left one of the bullets in Saucerman's leg. This war memento has remained with him ever since.

Saucerman was airlifted on a C-47 to Guam where he stayed for a week and received some blood transfusions. Then he was transported to the Naval Hospital in Pearl Harbor, Hawaii. His cast was cut off and he was put into a traction bed to help his leg heal properly.

He continued with his recuperation at the Navy Hospital in Oakland, CA where he stayed through the summer of 1945, laying on his lower back in another body cast. His older brother, Dean (the Marine who had served earlier in the war with the 1st Marine Division), had settled in Northern California and was able to visit with him. As Saucerman's leg healed he was able to get around on crutches and spent some weekends at his brother's home.

He completed his convalescence in Santa Cruz, CA and was finally discharged from the Marine Corps on December 13th, 1945. He left the Marines with a Purple Heart and the pride of knowing that he had served his nation in combat.

Saucerman returned to Indiana, where he worked for the state conservation department for a few years and then labored as a carpenter in Sullivan County before landing a job at Allison's GM in Indianapolis, working as a tool and gauge inspector. He retired in 1986 after 35 years.

In 1950, Sacuerman met his future wife, Lois Davis (also from Sullivan County). They were married April 3, 1953 and enjoyed 58 years together before her death in 2011. They raised two sons: Darrell and Gary and were blessed with four grandchildren.

Lois Davis.

Wayne displays a LIFE article on the Iwo Jima Battle that features a photo of him (see enlargement at left).

Today the 89-year-old Saucerman lives in rural Monrovia, Indiana and enjoys spending time with his family. The bullet in his leg is always present and reminds him of a brutal war fought almost 70 years ago. It also reminds him that he was blessed enough to survive the battle and enjoy a wonderful life that his and others' sacrifice have made possible.

Driving Across the Islands
Veteran Recalls His Service in the Pacific Theater

The Pacific Ocean is a vast body of water dotted with more than 25,000 islands. During World War II, Army veteran Adrain Stanger got to know eight of those islands very well as he drove across them in his ton and a half truck.

Born in Crown Center, Indiana on December 19, 1921, Stanger was the oldest of six children raised by his parents, Carl and Garnet Stanger. He grew up in Martinsville, Indiana and, except for his three years in World War II, has lived there ever since.

After completing his freshman year at Martinsville High School, he dropped out and began working full-time at a sawmill in Paragon. From that point on Stanger recalled, "I never was without a job."

On July 23, 1942, at the age of 20, he was drafted into the Army. He was inducted at Fort Benjamin Harrison in Indianapolis. Stanger reported to Camp Stoneman in Northern CA on August 6th and, within days, was on his way to Hawaii with the Army's 40th Infantry Division to protect the islands from further Japanese assault.

He underwent some hasty combat and bayonet training and was then assigned as a truck driver with the 115th Combat Engineer Battalion, Company B.

Stanger was assigned to drive a ton and a half truck. "It was B-14," he said, recalling the truck's identification tag painted on the front left bumper. "It didn't have any doors; just cutouts where the doors would have been."

He got plenty of driving practice. "I went somewhere every day", he remembered. Most of the time he was hauling men or pulling a trailer across the islands as the

Adrain (center) and his buddies on his service truck in Hilo City, Hawaii, where they placed gun emplacements around the shoreline.

division trained for building roads and bridges. "I drove over 12,000 miles," he said of his year plus time on Hawaii, Oahu and Maui.

The division left Hawaii in December of 1943 and arrived at Guadalcanal for further training and combat patrols. Some Japanese forces were still on the other side of the island.

"It was the rat hole of the Pacific!" Stanger said! "Worst island I was ever on! It was awful hot and muggy, and the mosquitoes were horrible. We had to put mosquito netting over us in the tents."

It wasn't just the weather that made life so miserable for the division. It was the road conditions as well. "Fighting the mud was terrible," Stanger recalled of his driving missions of moving ammunition between storage facilities. His truck would get stuck, but fortunately it was a four-wheel drive so he was able to work himself out of the mess most of the time. They hauled lava from the volcanoes to put on the roads in place of gravel.

The truck drivers used paint to blacken in the headlights to where there was only a 2"x1/4" slit to keep from being seen. The men did the same with the light bulbs in rooms where they were staying, except for a small round hole on the very bottom.

A few months later, on April 23rd, the Division moved to Cape Gloucester on New Britton Island. For the next seven months Stanger drove his truck primarily in support of his unit's building project to convert a house into an emergency hospital.

Adrain in front of Jeep.

On December 9th, the 40th Division was on the move again. This time, their destination was the Philippine Islands. They landed at Lingayen Gulf in Luzon on January 9, 1945 under assault by the Japanese. "The Japs bombed us our whole way in," Stanger recalled. "Two or three in our company were killed and others were injured."

Once again, Stanger took to his truck, hauling his squad to different points on the island as they closed in on the Japanese occupiers.

Once Luzon was brought under control, the 40th Division moved combat operations to the Paney Islands and later to Los Negros Island. There was minimal resistance. They were on Los Negros Island when the war ended in August with the surrender of Japan.

Stanger had enough points to leave for home as soon as the war ended. He boarded a troop transport and spent 30 days traveling back across the Pacific Ocean. The ship went through the Panama Canal and Stanger got to get off the ship and walk the land along the canal. The ship finally arrived back to its homeport in Virginia.

Adrain and Vivian with Robert and Richard.

Upon his return to the United States he went to Ft. Leonardwood, Missouri, then to Atlanta, Nebraska and was discharged in Topeka, Kansas.

Stanger spent a total of three years in the Army. His time overseas in Foreign Service was 2 years, 10 months, and 20 days. His time in-state was 3 months and 12 days. He left military service with the Asiatic Pacific Theater medal/ribbon with 3 bronze battle stars, a Good Conduct ribbon, Philippine Liberation ribbon with a bronze star, 5 overseas service bars and one service stripe. He returned home to Martinsville, where he came across a schoolmate that he had known but never dated. Her name was Vivian (Burkett) Blunk. She had married a serviceman who had been killed in action while serving in Germany. And she had two young sons by him.

Stanger didn't waste any time taking her and the boys under his wing. The two of them fell in love and were married on February 14, 1946. Together they raised Robert and Richard and then went on to have four of their own children: Tom, Melissa, Shannon and Kip.

Stanger worked at a filling station and did some other odd jobs for a few years before he was hired at a body shop in Martinsville where he worked for 25 years. He then worked in maintenance at Blue Cross Blue Shield (Indianapolis) for 10 years before retiring in 1986 at the age of 65.

Stanger and his wife enjoyed almost 40 years of camping together. They owned several different campers and even had a motorhome. "She loved it," Stanger said with fond memories of traveling with his wife across the country.

Vivian died in October of 2011, but not before the couple got to celebrate their 65th wedding anniversary.

Stanger has been an active member in the Martinsville community. He has been a member of the VFW Post for 51 years (serving as Post Commander for two terms in the 1970s), the American Legion for 48 years, the Masonic Lodge for 63 years and he has been an active member of Baptist Tabernacle Church.

He has kept busy around his house as well, mowing his own lawn up until this past year.

The 93-year-old Stanger still does some fishing. But mostly he enjoys spending time with his family and remembering with fondness a lifetime spent in Martinsville and a 66-year marriage to the love of his life.

And occasionally he thinks back to the only years he ever lived beyond Martinsville, Indiana, to a time when he was a young man serving his country in the South Pacific from the cab of a truck.

Adrain Stanger, 2014.

From Killing to Kindness
A Marine's Combat and Friendship Experience with the Japanese

Like many young men his age following the attack on Pearl Harbor, Herman Strakis left the family farm behind and headed off to war. The young man, born on June 22, 1922, wanted to "kill the Japs." In a twist of irony, three years later he would end his long and violent combat experience actually offering and experiencing friendship with the Japanese on their home soil.

Originally from Olivet, South Dakota, the Strakis family had moved to Palmer, Indiana after the Depression to be closer to family and to start a dairy farm. Following the attack on Pearl Harbor, Herman's older brothers left for the war while Herman stayed home and tended the farm. But the younger Strakis soon heard his own call to duty and enlisted on December 14th, 1942. As there were no sons left to help run the dairy farm, the family put it up for an auction sale and moved to Indianapolis.

TRAINING

Herman arrived in San Diego and began the ten weeks of boot camp to become a U.S. Marine. "They scared me," he said, referring to the drill instructors. "I was just a dumb farm kid!"

After Boot Camp Liberty (Herman at left).

Following boot camp, he was assigned to the Weapon's Section of Kilo Company, in the 3rd Battalion, 6th Marine Regiment, 2nd Marine Division. He and others assigned to that unit were then sent to Tank School. They trained for combat operations with tank support at a place called Jacques Farm Camp, which was located 3 miles south of the main camp.

Unlike the main camp where the infantry regiments stayed, these other camps were predominately tent camps, although Herman's group actually stayed in a barn out in a field. It was here that Strakis qualified as a machine gunner and became a squad leader. He learned all about fighting with tanks. But for all the training he received, he would never see or use an Allied tank throughout the battles of the Pacific War.

The 2nd Division left U.S. soil on Mother's Day, 1943 and headed for the South Pacific. After 6 months of jungle warfare training on New Zealand, the men of the 2nd Marine Division were ready for combat.

THE BATTLE ON TARAWA

Herman's first battle experience was on the island of Tarawa. On November 20th, 1943 the Marines of the 2nd Division climbed down the cargo nets of their

Landing Ships (LST's) and into the waiting Higgins boats to ferry them to the shore. The trip was supposed to take half an hour or less, but a mistake on figuring the tide schedule stranded the men in their cramped boats for 19 hours as they waited for the tide to come back in.

When they finally did get close enough to shore, the Marines filed out of the boats and into the water. They were greeted by rounds of ammunition fired from the Japanese soldiers who were dug in around the island. Danger came not only from the rounds whizzing by the men but from the water as well. Herman recalled, "There I was loaded with 90 pounds of gear to carry. We had weighed ourselves before taking off

Crowded Higgins boat.

for Tarawa. We walked out of the front ramp of the Higgins boat and into the water, which was waist level. Suddenly, I walked into a shell hole. The tracers are coming toward us, so our heads were close to the water so that we would be less a target. I walk into that shell hole and by golly I walked clean over my head! I couldn't swim a lick if I wanted because of all that gear I had on me. You just had to walk as quickly as you could across the hole, gobbling up some sea water as you move, until your feet come out of the hole and your head can break the surface of the water again." The Marines had to negotiate 200 yards as rounds were fired at them and as the craters left by shells threatened to drown them.

As the men got closer to shore they saw the bodies of injured and dead Marines all over the place. They passed through the bodies as they came ashore. "There was red hot fire all the time, as we reached the island", Herman recalled.

After a few hours of intense fighting, darkness approached. Herman and the other Marines were instructed to find some cover for the night. Herman jumped into a shell hole and, to his great horror, discovered he wasn't alone. He recalled, "I jumped into that shell hole and BLAZES! There was a Japanese soldier lying there!

US Marines resting near an amphibian tractor, Tarawa, Gilbert Islands, Nov. 1943.

We had been told to treat dead Japanese soldiers as is if they were still alive because they often faked death in order to kill more Allied Forces. I was scared of him as I could be. I stayed awake the whole night long and the next morning I could see he hadn't moved. So I was happy that I didn't have to shoot him. But I was ready if need be."

The fighting on Tarawa was brief but furious. The whole campaign lasted only 75 hours. But by the end of the 3 days of fighting the Marines had killed almost all of the 4,500 Japanese soldiers defending the island. The Marines lost over 1,000 of their own men — including Herman's good friend, Glenn Trout. Glenn was killed on Thanksgiving Day by a Japanese sniper while he was walking next to Herman. He was buried, along with many other fallen Marines, in the sands of Tarawa. Now, with the death of his buddy, Herman had another reason — a much more personal one — to exact his revenge on the Japanese.

After the Tarawa campaign, 2nd Division returned to the big island of Hawaii. They settled at Camp Tarawa to undergo more training and get some fresh replacements. After a few months stay, the division again traversed the Pacific Ocean for their next major combat mission. This one would be on the island of Saipan.

BATTLE ON SAIPAN

Located in the Mariana Island Chain in the Western Pacific, Saipan was a key last line of defense for the Japanese homeland and, as such, was to be protected at all costs. Some 30,000 Japanese troops were there to defend the island from Allied attack.

"In every direction that you looked the sea was filled with LST's," recalled Herman, as they neared Saipan.

At midnight of June 15th, 1944 the Marines on board the LST's (Landing Ship Tank) enjoyed an all-you-can-eat pre-combat breakfast of eggs, biscuits/gravy, bacon, toast, juice and coffee. At about 0200 (2 am) Herman and the other Marines from his battalion got inside their LVT's (Landing Vehicles Tracked) that had been parked in the lower hull of the ship. Herman's company, K Company, was in front and would be the first wave of tanks going ashore. Herman's tank was in the very first row. He would lead.

As the LVT's left the mother ship they were huddled underneath the large battleships that were firing their big guns to soften up the island just before the Marines landed. Herman recalled the damage done to his ears from the noise and concussion of the big guns of the battleships: "We were right under those 105 mm howitzers and they go off and you're under there bobbing around in water, and I could feel my ears ring … both of them... they're still ringing to this very minute from that day forward. It has not stopped at all. The sound is the same as it was almost 70 years ago."

Herman was assigned as one of the turret gunners on his LVT. He and the other gunner were the only two men allowed to have their heads over the protection of the LVT's heavy metal frame. They approached the island in rows of 12-15 tanks and were taking heavy fire from the Japanese. As they were in the first wave and everyone else was behind them, Herman felt the rest of the men were counting on this first row of LVT's to clear out the enemy. Herman recalled: "We were firing our machine guns during the approach. During training we had been instructed to use single trigger pull bursts of 3 rounds at a time. So much fear gripped us now that we were firing off our belt of 150 rounds on just 2 finger pull bursts. The barrel of the machine guns got so hot that the weapons would keep firing, even after our fingers had been taken off the triggers."

As the vehicle moved toward land, a Marine officer got up beside Herman to look out of the metal slit in the turret that was used to aim the machine gun. Herman recalled, "He got up there with his chin on my shoulder and our helmets touching

Marines take cover behind a M4 Sherman tank while clearing Japanese forces from the northern end of the island of Saipan. 8 July 1944.

so that he could see the action. He no more got up there than a bullet came right through the narrow slot in the steel shield and hit him in the head. He collapsed dead on my shoulder. I laid him down on the deck so that I could keep firing."

Upon reaching the shore, Herman and the other machine gunners on the LVT's had to point the nozzle of their machine guns straight up in the air because the guns were still firing off rounds, even with no pull on the trigger.

Another close call with death awaited Herman on land. He had made it up to a sand bank and was taking cover from enemy fire when a Japanese hand grenade landed on the sand bank slightly above him. Herman had just a split second to turn his face into the sand and shield his head with the back of his hand. Thankfully, the explosion of the grenade went up and out, sparing Herman most of the impact and shrapnel. He received some cuts on his head and hands, but no serious injury. His life was spared, and he became a Purple Heart recipient for the wounds that he sustained.

"Someone from our group got hit every day," Herman recalled. "We just bandaged each other up and kept fighting."

At around 2 a.m. that first night on Saipan, Herman was suddenly awakened from his shallow sleep inside a shell hole. Their squad leader, a Gunnery Sergeant John Mustacelli from Hudson, PA was calling out for his Marines to get into battle position. Japanese tanks, which had been concealed during the Allied landing, suddenly were advancing upon the Marines in a surprise night attack. There were more than 20 of the tanks careening down upon the Marines.

The Gunnery Sergeant instructed the members of his squad team to quickly move beyond (behind) the tanks so that so that they could shoot at the advancing Japanese soldiers. The squads of Marines had to move forward in between the blasts of fire from the tanks. They hit the decks for cover when they anticipated the tanks firing and advanced while the tanks reloaded — a tricky and extremely dangerous guesswork that resulted in some tragic fatalities.

Herman recalled being next to Gunny Sergeant Mustacelli as they advanced on the tanks. Both of them dove down to the sand as they anticipated the gunfire from the tank ahead of them. The Gunny was a fraction of a second late in getting to the ground. He was ahead of Herman and Herman was on the ground with his head between the Gunny's legs. When Herman stood up during the reload of the tank he discovered that the Gunny had been hit by the tank round. "It blew out his insides", Herman recalled as he choked up with tears.

Gunny Mustacelli.

The battle lasted for 24 days and finally came to an end on July 9th, as the Allied troops secured the island in victory. It was, however, a costly victory! Of their 71,000 troops that landed, over 3,400 Allies were killed and over 10,000 injured. Among those killed in action was another friend of Herman's, Hoot Gibson, as well as the Gunnery Sergeant of Herman's company. The fatalities were much worse for the Japanese. Of their 31,000 soldiers, 25,000 perished and 5,000 committed suicide.

Killing did, however, finally give way to kindness as the battle drew down. Herman and some other Marines came across 6 women and children island inhabitants that had been hiding out in a cave. "We offered them what little we had to eat", he said. "We had only instant coffee but nothing to really feed them with. But they would take that raw coffee powder and just eat the sack and all. They were so surprised and amazed that we didn't shoot them. After an hour of talking to settle them down while waiting for them to be handed over to other authorities those people were almost laughing with joy that no one shot anybody. They had always been told that we would murder them no matter what, so they should never give up."

Following their victory, the 2nd Marine Division set up a base camp on Saipan. Here the Marines lived, trained and jumped off for more island campaigns. There was mop up duty on the island of Tinian, followed by participation in a mock landing at Okinawa, which was designed to draw the Japanese away from the actual landing location of the Marines and the Army.

OCCUPATION DUTY IN JAPAN

While living on Saipan, Herman's friend, Dick Eubanks came down with malaria. Herman wrote letters home to Dick's parents during his illness. He also had to watch out for his own life. Dick's high fevers caused some fits of rage where he pointed his gun and threatened to kill Herman. "He was scary as the devil", remembered Herman.

After the atomic bombs were dropped on Hiroshima (August 6, 1945) and Nagasaki (August 9, 1945), the Japanese finally surrendered. Although the war came to an end, the work of the 2nd Marine Division was not yet done. They were assigned occupation duty at Nagasaki.

Arriving on September 22, 1945, Herman recalled the warning given to him by his Marine leaders that they would probably not live past the age of 60 due to the radiation they would be exposed to at Nagasaki. Looking back, Herman realized the truth behind the warning. Most of his fellow Marine buddies did start dying off at age 60.

Herman (back row with shirt open) and other Marines on Saipan.

Occupation duty at Nagasaki.

The first couple of days in Nagasaki they were quite confused, not knowing what to do, as there were no officers around. But they eventually received some guidance and life settled into a routine of guard duty and walking around assigned areas of the city. Herman's group was assigned near the big fuel tanks of the Mitsubishi Steel Mill that had been reduced to rubble and debris after the bomb. During guard duty Herman and the other Marines didn't even need to carry their rifles. There was no resistance and no trouble from the citizens.

It was during guard duty on Nagasaki that Herman met a Japanese man who worked as a security guard for one of the big fuel tanks located near the area where the Marines were staying. The two of them visited together on several occasions during their guard duty and became quite friendly with one another. Herman recalled, "There was absolutely no animosity or hard feelings between us. We visited like old friends. I'll tell you, the feeling was so strongly friendly that you could almost hug one another because you were so happy to see something besides killing!" Indeed, kindness was something far more powerful than killing.

One very humorous incident occurred during his time in Nagasaki. As Herman remembers it, "When we got one of the buildings cleared up to where we lived in them as our tent area, we piped in water from on the top of the hill, outside the building. It looked like about a 2-inch iron black pipe. They drilled holes and put it on a tripod alongside of the building in an alleyway. Word was out that 2 p.m. tomorrow we get to shower. It was the first shower we really got. So they turned the water loose on that two-inch pipe. I'm on the third floor watching to see what will happen. Information had gotten out that they were going to turn the water on. And here come a bunch of people (citizens of Nagasaki) with pots, pans and everything else. All of our guys are out there standing, taking a shower. And here comes these people with pots and pans, and they walk right into the shower area and catch the fresh water. And our people about killed themselves trying to get back into the building. They run and jump and go like crazy. Everybody is naked as a jaybird. And the Japanese men and women alike, they could care less about it. They let them run all around. But you know what? Three days later, our guys just stayed there. They would stand there and shower and women could stand there right next to them with a pot catching water. And nobody gave a hoot! All the modesty went out the window in three days time! We'd become friendly people!"

As the Marines got ready to leave Japan and return home in November, there was a final act of kindness as some of the residents of Nagasaki gave Herman and other Marines 25 mm Japanese rifles as a going home present.

RETURN HOME

On January 6th, 1946 Herman's three-year combat odyssey came to a close as he returned stateside and was discharged. During his time of service, he had spent 2 years, 6 months and 25 days deployed to the Pacific theater of war. He left the Marines with a Purple Heart and a Good Conduct Medal.

Herman standing with a car.

After returning to his family in Indianapolis, Herman took over running the 423-acre family farm. Back problems — he had injured his back while on Saipan — forced him to look for a different vocation. After working on cars for a while, Herman took a class at the Reppert School of Auctioneering and had a successful career as an auctioneer in Central Indiana for the next 50+ years, often volunteering his services and raising millions of dollars for favorite charities and organizations. He was chosen as Indiana Auctioneer of the Year in 1982.

Herman married his first wife, Nadine, on January 26, 1946. Together they raised four children: Cathie (1946), Russell (1948), George (1950) and Connie (1952). Nadine died in 1985. Three years later, in 1988, Herman married Jackie Tilkins and enjoyed twenty years with her until her death in 2008.

Herman and Nadine at Speedway in 1947.

In 2010, Mary Reynolds became his wife. The couple continues to live at the house Herman built in Southwestern Indianapolis.

Herman, Nadine and their children in the 1950s.

Herman in 2012 with Purple Heart.

It has been a full life for the 92-year-old veteran. There are memories of killing during combat as a young man. But thankfully, in his lifetime there have been far more memories of kindnesses received and offered.

Vehicle Man

Veteran focused on vehicles in war and in life

Paul Thacker has been around vehicles his entire life. The Martinsville, Indiana native had 3 different cars before he turned 16. Little did he realize at that young age that the rest of his life would revolve around vehicles — both in war as well as in peacetime.

Born David Paul Thacker on January 26, 1921 in rural Martinsville, he was the youngest of four children born to his parents. His father died when he was just 18 months old. But he had a wonderful stepfather, who had served in World War I and loved young Paul as his own.

Thacker attended school up through the 9th grade and then worked full-time as a farmer.

He was drafted into the U.S. Army on November 4, 1942 at the age of 21. Two weeks later he reported to Ft. Benjamin Harrison for military processing.

Thacker did his military training at Ft. Bliss in El Paso, TX. He was assigned to the 362nd Anti-aircraft Search and Light Radar Battalion. But most of his work was as a driver for the different commanders of Bravo Company. In his years of service he drove three different jeeps and served four different company commanders.

"I loved it!" Thacker recalled. "I never put a scratch on any of the three jeeps I drove. I took good care of them."

Thacker's unit left for the South Pacific in the summer of 1943. The troop transport ship he was on had limited water. He recalled, "The captain of the ship said he only had enough water for the crew to take showers. We went 29 days without a shower!"

Paul poses with his family in front of their car.

Paul as young man.

Their destination was the island of Guadalcanal. But before reaching it, the ship caught on fire and had to make a repair stop on the island of New Caledonia. Thacker spent his two weeks there working in the rations dumps (a supply depot for resupplying all the islands to the north). He slept under a canopy in the open muddy fields while waiting for the ship to be repaired.

The ship arrived at Guadalcanal on July 13, 1943. Later that evening, as Thacker and the others were sleeping on the beach, Jap planes dropped their skip bombs on the ship, which resulted in terrible explosions and the death of many of the Seabees who were unloading the ship.

"I was scared to death," Thacker remembered. "We were all just boys. I remember thinking, 'What in the world did we get into?'"

What they had gotten into was a hellish place of discomfort and danger. By day, Thacker drove his company commander around the island in the 120-degree heat, trying to avoid the attention of Japanese snipers. At night he tried to sleep but was always uncomfortably warm and only too aware of the danger lurking around him. The Japanese were hiding out on the island and often made surprise attacks against the Allies in the darkness of night. Thacker recalled, "We lived in total darkness at night for a year. We couldn't have any lights. There were still Japanese snipers out there."

When they weren't being harassed by ground troops, Japanese planes dropping bombs often interrupted their sleep. There were frequent mad dashes to the limited protection of foxholes.

Paul on Bivouac at Ft. Bliss, TX.

Thacker and his unit spent 17 months in the oppressive heat, frequent rain, and muddy conditions on constant alert for Japanese attacks.

While Thacker was driving his company commander from place to place others from his unit were using their powerful searchlight to guide planes in for night landings at Henderson Field. "Our searchlight was 52 million candle power," recalled Thacker. "We could pick a plane up 12 miles out and lead it in (for a landing)."

Following their 17 months at Guadalcanal, Thacker and his unit served in New Guinea for four months before moving on to the Philippines, where Thacker served as a Combat MP (Military Policeman) and drove around the city of Manila on patrol for three months.

In August of 1945, Thacker left Manila and was headed home when the atomic bombs were dropped on Japan, essentially ending World War II.

"We all kissed the ground when we got off the ship," he recalled, remembering his safe arrival in San Francisco.

Thacker returned home and drove a semi-truck, hauling bricks

Paul driving a Jeep at Fort Bliss.

Paul with the Chevrolet Certified Technician Plague recognizing him for 33 years of service.

for a year. He then got a job with Chevrolet Truck Body in Indianapolis, working as a truck mechanic for 33 years. His final job before retiring was serving as a mechanic at the Morgantown Gas Station.

While his vocation was "fueled" by cars, his love was fueled by one Monta Rose Hacker, whom he had met at the Paragon Homecoming Festival on Labor Day of 1947. The couple married that same December. Their marriage was blessed with a daughter, Jacqueline. Later 2 grandchildren and 5 great-grandchildren were added to their family. In 2012 the couple celebrated their 65th wedding anniversary.

Thacker died on July 29, 2013 at the age of 92. He was buried with military honors at New South Park Cemetery in Martinsville, Indiana. He was a proud member of V.F.W. Post 1257.

Acknowledgements

There are many people who played a part in supporting this writing project.

I thank my sister, Linda for encouraging me to pursue my interest in writing at a time of career transition. Her affirmation gave me courage to try.

I owe special thanks to Brian Culp, editor of the Martinsville *Reporter Times* and *Mooresville-Decatur Times* newspapers. Without his willingness to begin publishing my stories in his newspapers I would likely have never pursued interviewing so many veterans and writing a book. I especially thank him for giving me permission to use the stories that he purchased from me and printed in his newspapers.

Thanks also go out to Kathy Linton of the *Hendricks County Flyer* for likewise printing some of my veteran stories in her newspaper.

Tawnee Hinton, a former church member of mine and a Navy Reserve Officer colleague, graciously provided me with her editing services. Thank you, Tawnee.

Robin Surface of Fideli Publishing provided me with her professional expertise as a book publisher. Words, sentences and paragraphs are the heart of a book. But if they are not formatted into an appealing layout and sandwiched between an attractive and eye-catching cover, most will never choose to read the book. Thanks for making this book attractive to readers, Robin.

Grant Thompson, director of the Indy Honor Flight organization, also gave me his encouragement and assistance in capturing veteran stories. I direct the reader to learning more about this awesome organization by reviewing the pages that describe it in the Introduction on pages xiii-xv of this book.

There are also some sponsors that I want to acknowledge. When I first came upon the idea of publishing a book, I considered self-publishing and financing the venture through corporate and individual sponsorship. Securing adequate sponsorship proved to be more difficult than I had thought, so I eventually gave up on the concept; but not before receiving some financial support from several businesses and 23 individuals and families. The business sponsors appear at the end of Art Brown's story. And the individual sponsors, who specifically supported the stories of Carl Marsh, Paul Maves and Herman Strakis, appear at the end of this Acknowledgement. I thank them for their support and for wanting to honor our veterans.

My good personal friends, Reid Reasor and Rob Grondahl, also offered me their encouragement during this process. I benefitted much from their support. And I continue to be blessed by their friendship and love.

I especially want to thank my daughter, Karlie for spending a day with me last summer and taking photographs of local veteran memorials for possible inclusion in this volume. I am grateful for her time and support in this venture. Her photos appear on pages viii, x, and 144.

I would be remiss if I did not thank you, the readers, for purchasing the book and reading the stories of these brave veterans from World War II. In an age where we spend a lot of time and money watching action movies about imaginary heroes defeating villains, it is encouraging to see that some of us know where to look for the true heroes of recent history.

And finally, I thank the veterans who dared to let me inside their homes to ask my personal questions of them. Some of their memories were unpleasant and still very emotional. I appreciate their courage to remember and to share their recollections with me. There would be no book without their willing participation. Most of the veterans did not know me before the interview, yet all of them were gracious and accommodating to me. I very much appreciate their willingness to share their service stories with me. I hope what I have written of them honors their incredible contribution to our nation's involvement in the World War II saga.

INDIVIDUAL AND FAMILY SPONSORS

Bob & Nancy Abernathy

Michael & Carol Albert

Doug & Lori Behrmann

Bob & Peggy Boyer

Chuck & Joyce Bowling

Walt & Liz Dieckamp

Jason & Nanci Duigou

Derek & Amy Eaton

Betty Hiday

Ron & Karen Homeier

George & Anna Leonard

Bob & Margo Martin

Ann Michael

Jean Minneman

Marie Olson

Rolla & Lynda Pruett

Tom & Kris Rafferty

Kevin & Judy Scheiwe

Bill & Annette Stoneking

Ron & Barb Stoner

Dennis & Shara Toole

Larry & Joyce Zimmerman

About the Author

Chaplain Ronald P. May

A native of Erie, Pennsylvania, Ron May has served as a Chaplain, Pastor and Freelance Writer. Following graduation from college and seminary he spent 23 years in full-time ministry as a Lutheran Pastor and 22 years in part-time ministry as a Navy Reserve Chaplain.

In 2012 he began work as a freelance writer, submitting the stories of military veterans and senior citizens for publication in local newspapers. The idea of writing a book on the life stories of veterans came to him while he was helping to preserve the military stories of four particular veterans.

Ron currently serves as Chaplain at Hoosier Village Retirement Community in Zionsville, Indiana and as a Hospice Chaplain at Paradigm Living Concepts in Indianapolis. When he isn't writing or serving as a chaplain, Ron can be found on a bicycle exploring Central Indiana or on the gridiron officiating high school football games each fall.

If you would like to correspond with Ron or arrange to have him as a guest speaker you can contact him by email at yourlifestory@live.com or by phone at 317-435-7636. You can also find him on the internet at www.lifestorybooks.net or follow him on Facebook.

CPSIA information can be obtained at www.ICGtesting.com
Printed in the USA
LVOW01s1737121015

457942LV00005B/5/P